Scroll Saw Art

Scroll Saw Art
Realistic Pictures in Wood

Patrick Spielman

Kerry Shirts

Sterling Publishing Co., Inc. New York
A Sterling/Chapelle Book

Chapelle Ltd.

Owner: Jo Packham

Editor: Leslie Ridenour / Gina Swapp

Staff: Marie Barber, Ann Bear, Areta Bingham, Kass Burchett, Rebecca Christensen, Marilyn Goff, Holly Hollingsworth, Susan Jorgensen, Barbara Milburn, Linda Orton, Karmen Quinney, Cindy Stoeckl

Photographer: Kevin Dilley for Hazen Photography

Acknowledgments by Kerry Shirts: I would like to thank the many dear friends and supportive family members who have so unselfishly helped with this book. Thanks to our technical illustrator, Roxanne Lemoine. Special thanks to my incredible wife, Charlotte, for her honest critiques and unfailing love. She keeps me young at heart and mind. Hey honey, here's the book!

Library of Congress Cataloging-in-Publication Data

Spielman, Patrick E.
   Scroll saw art / Patrick Spielman, Kerry Shirts
     p.cm.
   "A Sterling/Chapelle book."
   ISBN 0-8069-2897-2
   1. Jig saws. 2. Woodwork--Patterns. I. Shirts, Kerry. II. Title.

TT186.S6677 2000
745.51'3--dc21

00-027988

10 9 8 7 6 5 4 3 2 1

A Sterling/Chapelle Book

Published by Sterling Publishing Company, Inc.
387 Park Avenue South, New York, NY 10016
© 2000 by Chapelle Ltd.
Distributed in Canada by Sterling Publishing
% Canadian Manda Group, One Atlantic Avenue, Suite 105
Toronto, Ontario, Canada M6K 3E7
Distributed in Great Britain and Europe by Cassell PLC
Wellington House, 125 Strand, London WC2R 0BB, England
Distributed in Australia by Capricorn Link (Australia) Pty Ltd.
P.O. Box 6651, Baulkham Hills, Business Centre, NSW 2153, Australia
Printed in China
All Rights Reserved

Sterling ISBN 0-8069-2897-2

Due to the limited amount of space available, we must print our patterns at a reduced size in order to give our patrons the maximum number of patterns possible in our publications. We believe the quality and quantity of our patterns will compensate for any inconvenience this may cause.

If you have any questions or comments, please contact:

Chapelle Ltd., Inc.
P.O. Box 9252
Ogden, UT 84409
Phone: (801) 621-2777
FAX: (801) 621-2788
e-mail: chapelle@chapelleltd.com
website: www.chapelleltd.com

Pat Spielman can be reached via e-mail:
spielman@mail.wiscnet.net
or website: www.spielmanpatrick.com

Kerry Shirts can be reached via e-mail:
shirtail@cyberhighway.net
or website: www.cyberhighway.net/~shirtail

About the Authors

Patrick Spielman

Patrick Spielman lives surrounded by forest in the famous tourist area of Door County in northeast Wisconsin. A graduate of the University of Wisconsin-Stout, he taught high school and vocational woodworking in Wisconsin public schools for 27 years.

Today, he and his wife, Patricia, own Spielman's Wood Works and Spielman's Kid Works. Both are gift galleries that offer high-quality hand- and machine-crafted wood products produced locally and from around the world.

Patrick left the school classroom more than 10 years ago, but he continues to teach and share ideas through his published works. He enjoys consulting and lending his knowledge of woodworking to promote the talent and activities of other artisans. He has written more than 50 woodworking books with some translated into Dutch and German.

Kerry Shirts

Kerry has been involved with art in one form or another all his life. His mother taught him to draw. As a teenager, Kerry took art classes and credits an art instructor, Alice Foster, for being a phenomenal influence on his continued interest in art. When Kerry was 15 years old, his grandfather financed oil painting lessons. This background assists him in creating realistic-looking portraits in wood.

Kerry has been scroll sawing since 1990. He bought several scroll saw pattern books and cut many of those patterns. Then he decided to try something different. Instead of predrilling, cutting out pieces, and leaving them out, he decided to leave them in the project. One day he had glued inside pieces on a project and was called away. When he returned, they had glued unevenly, some pieces actually sitting high in the background, others recessed. In this, he noticed dimensional qualities. He then cut other patterns and stained them different colors to mimic shading. His technique has been refined to create realistic-looking animals or people.

As he saws, Kerry listens to his favorite music or books on tape. He received his B.S. in history from Idaho State University in 1994.

Kerry's art has been featured in art galleries in Jackson Hole, Wyoming; Yellowstone Park; Carmel, California; and Sun Valley, Idaho. Kerry features his work on the internet and has sold portraits internationally. He is also featured in many private collections around the United States.

Contents

Chapter 1　Tools & Materials

Chapter 2　Basic Techniques

Chapter 3　Beginner Projects

Chapter 4 Intermediate Projects

Chapter 5 Expert Projects

Chapter 6 Gallery & Inspirational Pieces

Introduction

Scroll saw segmentation portraiture is a new and exciting technique that involves a combination of fundamental scroll sawing and wood staining procedures. The process enables any scroll saw artist capable of following a line to create realistic-looking, three-dimensional wooden portraits of objects, wildlife, and even likenesses of real people.

The sawing process involves nothing more than temporarily bonding a photocopy of the pattern to the wood and sawing the individual pieces as dictated by the pattern lines. Next, the individual pieces are stained or colored as also directed on the pattern and illustrated by the accompanying color photograph. The pieces are then reassembled with glue, with some pieces set at slight differences of relief, to create the "whole" picture.

The project selections in this book range from very elementary—involving just a few cut segments of simplistic shapes, to more advanced projects—consisting of hundreds of pieces in complex or highly detailed shapes. Generally, however, the processes and procedures are all essentially the same. The more complex projects simply require more time.

Like a beautiful oil painting, a scroll-sawn segmentation portrait in wood looks more realistic when viewed at some distance. Up close, the details may not make much sense, like the brushwork on the canvas of a fine art painting may look visually disconnected. However, when you step back a bit, all the colors, tones, textures,

Photo No. i-1 The pattern for this Staring Wolf is for the beginner but has wonderful detail. It does not have to be mounted to become a wonderful piece of art.

8

and shadows emerge as a wonderful, coherent image. By and large the more pieces and the greater the detail involved, the closer to photographic realism the whole becomes.

This book is intended to be both an instructional and a stimulating reference. Projects are provided in three categories: beginner, intermediate, and expert. A selection of 30 patterns are provided. The Staring Wolf design is provided for both beginner and intermediate categories. See Photos No. i-1 and No. i-2. A photo gallery is also provided.

The Big Horn Ram design is also provided in the beginner and intermediate categories, plus another pattern with even more detail is given in the expert category. See Photo No. i-3 on page 10.

These subjects show how effective a simple design can be and how it can be embellished to become more realistic in the intermediate and expert levels.

With the exception of the Fawn and the Leopard, very few inside cuts need to be made. Any size scroll saw capable of making consistently square, vertical cuts with commonly used blades is really the only tool necessary.

Photo No. i-2 An intermediate pattern for the Staring Wolf shows the additional detail that makes the wolf look even more realistic. It looks terrific in a wood frame.

The patterns also provide recommended staining instructions for coloring the individual pieces. The color intensity may vary due to the absorbency levels of different woods. There are no hard and fast rules in the staining process. When finished, your project will not be an exact duplication of the photograph in the book. It will, however, be a one-of-a-kind piece of dramatic art that is your own creation—one that very likely you or anyone else will never be able to duplicate exactly again. Therein lies the enjoyable experience of making realistic scroll saw segmentation portraiture.

Photo No. i-3 The pattern for this Big Horn Ram is for the more expert wood cutter and looks incredibly realistic. Notice how the intricate cuts provide more 3-D pieces and shadows.

The majority of the patterns will, however, need to be enlarged with a photocopy machine. You can make them any size desired. Where possible, the enlargement recommendations given for the patterns are close to life-size. You may also opt to miniaturize some of the beginner and intermediate project patterns.

The art you are capable of producing with these basic techniques is virtually unlimited. Have fun; expand your vision; think like an artist; and experiment with woods, stains, coloring, textures, and various backgrounds or plaque choices that will add to the dramatic effects of your efforts.

Chapter 1

Scroll Saws

The scroll saw is used to cut flat wood into distinct parts or segments. Almost any scroll saw that carries fine blades (and that includes most saws available today) can be used for portrait segmentation. This chapter provides essential information about scroll saws for the beginner and illustrates just a few of the more than 50 different machines on the market today.

When compared to all other power-driven devices that cut wood, the scroll saw is un-questionably the safest, most user-friendly, and easiest to master. Scroll sawing is enjoyed by crafters and artists of all ages. It requires no mechanical skills and it allows for safely cutting small pieces of wood to quickly make a variety of projects.

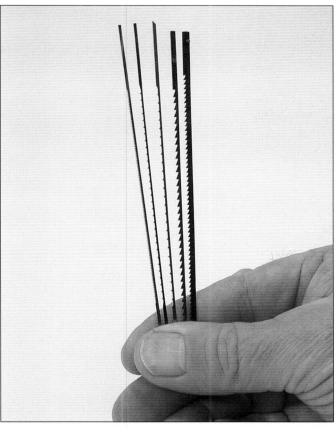

Photo No. 1-2 Scroll saws carry narrow blades. As a general rule, select narrower blades for making tight turns and wider blades for larger curves and thicker wood.

Photo No. 1-1 This low-priced 16" scroll saw is very popular in England, Europe, and the United States. It features up-front controls and variable-speed controls. It is sold with a Tradesman and Dremel label in the U.S. and as a Rexon in other countries. The U.S. price is under $200.

The major function of the scroll saw is to cut irregular curves and openings in flat wood. A very small, thin blade is held taut between the ends of two horizontal arms that move up and down in unison to create a reciprocating cutting motion. See Photos No. 1-1 and No. 1-2. The blade moves vertically through an opening in the saw table. The operator supports the work piece on the table and advances it into the blade in a manner that is similar to feeding fabric under the needle of a sewing machine.

Because of the narrow blades, extremely sharp arcs and turns can be cut to make highly detailed and intricate shapes. See Photo No. 1-3.

Scroll saws are available in a wide variety of prices, ranging from less than $100.00 to well over $2,000.00, with a growing list of features and options that improve the overall performance of the machine. There are many brands to choose from and some manufacturers offer several models. Before purchasing any scroll saw, seriously consider the full range of work that might be done with it in the future.

Photo No. 1-3 Here, typical portrait segments for the expert version of the Big Horn Ram project are being cut. All pieces are sawn free, working from the outside inward. This and most other projects do not require making inside cuts.

Scroll saws can cut a wide variety of materials, including various metals and plastics. Some scroll saws have more capability and capacity to saw thicker and larger sizes of wood than do others. Thus, it is necessary to investigate and try various saws, to see which saw best matches your overall long-term sawing needs. For a more in-depth description of scroll saw usage and features, the previously published Sterling books, *Scroll Saw Basics* and *Scroll Saw Handbook*, are recommended.

The size of the scroll saw is designated by its "throat capacity," or, the distance from the blade to the rear of the machine. A 15" saw, for example, can cut to the center of a 30"-diameter circle. Saw sizes range from 13" to 30" and are available in bench and floor model versions.

The rate at which the blade moves up and down in strokes per minute is called the "blade speed." The least expensive saws have just one constant speed. Two-speed and variable-speed

Photo No. 1-4 Ryobi's 16" variable-speed scroll saw costs about $180. Notice the lower vacuum port for dust extraction.

saws allow for better control when cutting thin or soft materials, as well as the ability to efficiently cut metal and plastic.

The photos included here provide a good overview of some popular brands of saws that are currently available. See Photos No. 1-4 through No. 1-10 this page and on page 14.

In addition to considering variable-speed saws, some features worth considering are up-front controls, i.e.: an on-off switch, blade tensioning, and blade speed adjustment. See Photo No. 1-11 on page 15. Look into adaptability, i.e.: the possibility of adding a light, a magnifier, a dust collector, and/or a blower. A foot switch is a good optional accessory. One important feature to look for is the saw's capability for changing blades quickly and/or threading the blade through the work piece easily for making inside cuts. See Photo No. 1-12 on page 15.

Photo No. 1-5 Delta's 16" scroll saw is available in two-speed and variable-speed versions. The cost is about $185.

Photo No. 1-6 This is a German-made 18" variable-speed Hegner with up-front tensioning. It costs about $1000.

13

Photo No. 1-7 DeWalt's Canadian-made 20" variable-speed saw has many innovative features. The cost is under $500.

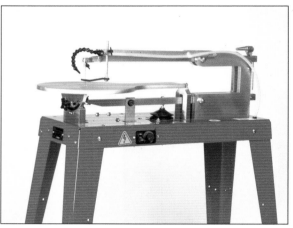

Photo No. 1-9 The RBI Hawk is a 26" variable-speed saw with up-front tensioning. It is U.S.-made and costs around $1200.

Photo No. 1-8 Canadian-made Excalibur's 30" variable-speed machine has the largest throat capacity available. The cost is about $1400.

Photo No. 1-10 The Eclipse, a U.S.-made 20" variable-speed scroll saw, is one of the newest major brand saws available. It has many exclusive design features such as up-front controls and a unique drive system that provides true vertical blade travel throughout a long 1½" stroke. The cost is about $1600.

Photo No. 1-11 The control panel of the Eclipse saw features on-off, variable-speed control, and light switches. It also has an hour meter that tells you how long a job takes.

Blades

Blades are fairly inexpensive, costing 20 to 75 cents each, depending upon size, style, quantity, and quality. The most popular blade is the 5" plain-end type. Sizes are designated by numbers and range from No. 2/0 and No. 0 in very fine, to No. 1, No. 2, and No. 4 in fine, to No. 5 to No. 7 in medium, and No. 8 to No.12 in large sizes. Photo No. 1-2 on page 11 illustrates some medium- and fine-sized blades. The slight forward and back movement of the blade during the cutting stroke of the scroll saw produces a cut surface that is very smooth and seldom needs sanding.

There are various blade tooth design configurations available, with skip-tooth being one of the most popular. See Drawing No. 1-1 on page 16. This blade tooth design provides for fast sawdust removal and provides cool and smooth cuts. Look for blades with reversed lower teeth. These minimize tear-out or splintering as the teeth exit the bottom surface of the work piece.

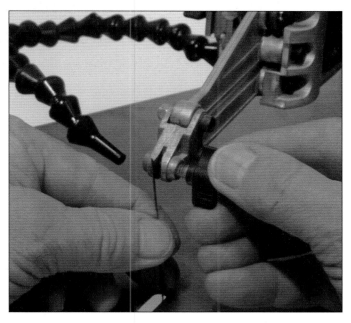

No. 1-12 An important feature for many scrolling jobs is easy-to-use blade clamps that permit quick blade changes, and an adjustable blower to direct sawdust away from the cutting line and the operator.

Less expensive blades have burr edges along one side. The burr edge is the result of material flow from stamping or milling during the manufacturing process. The burr-edged side of the blade is sharper and provides less cutting resistance than the burrless side of the blade. See Drawing No. 1-2.

This causes the blade to track slightly to one side while cutting—a condition for which one can quickly learn to compensate. The side-tracking tendency of these blades is especially noticeable when making straight line cuts.

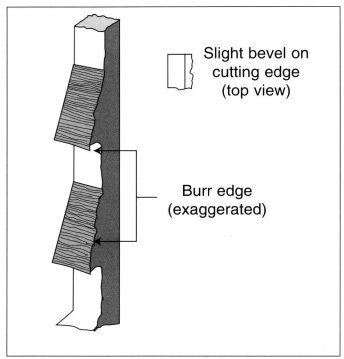

Drawing No. 1-2 This enlarged sketch shows the sharp, microscopic metal burr along one edge of the blade. This condition is typical of less expensive scroll saw blades. It is caused by the way the blades are manufactured. For this reason, scroll saw blades actually track unevenly, because there is more cutting resistance on one edge of the blade than the other.

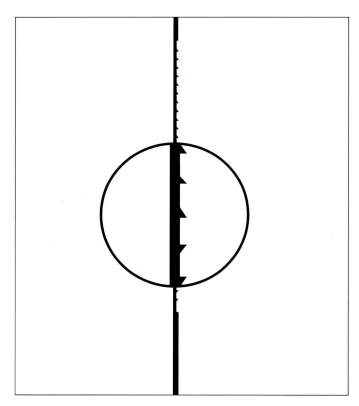

Drawing No. 1-1 Skip-tooth design with reversed lower teeth minimizes bottom splintering or feathering along the cut edges of the piece.

The best, newest, and most expensive blades are ground from tempered steel with abrasive wheels. These are known as "ground blades." They last longer and cut straighter when compared to other blades. Currently, they are only available in sizes No. 5, No.7, and No. 9.

Use ground blades for smooth cut surfaces. They stay sharp longer when cutting plywoods and also make smooth cuts in pine. Avoid spiral blades. Although designed to cut in all directions, they are not a good choice. They cut slowly, take a wide kerf, and leave a very rough-cut surface.

For cutting the beginner and intermediate level projects in this book, use a No. 5 blade. Use a No. 2 fine blade for the more detailed cuts that are required for the expert level projects.

Saw Preparation

Make certain to first read and review the owner's manual and observe all of the safety precautions relative to the use of the scroll saw. For all of the projects, it is necessary to make cuts with the saw table set square to the blade. Use a small square or protractor to make and check this adjustment. The factory calibrations on the blade-tilt scales of most scroll saws are difficult to read (especially with bifocals) and most are not accurate. See Photo No. 1-13. Make certain that the blade is installed with the teeth pointing downward. Tension it correctly, according to the manufacturer's instructions.

Wood Products

Silver maples and red maples are also known as soft maples, which are the recommended woods for making the projects in this book. Other light-colored species, however, can be substituted. Almost all of the projects in this book were cut from soft

Photo No. 1-13 Use a simple protractor to easily check the squareness of the table to the blade. This is the easiest way to get an accurate square measurement.

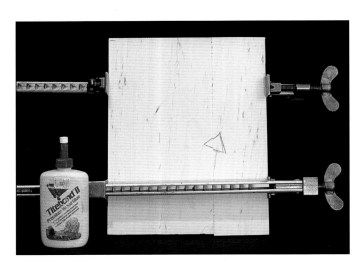

Photo No. 1-14 Glue narrow boards edge-to-edge to make wider panels.

uniformly. Thus, the color intensities can vary considerably. This is not entirely bad because in nature and wildlife there is also a wide variety of coloring and intensity. Heavier, denser woods are more difficult to work with when trying to obtain deep dark colors than with lighter, lower density woods. Sometimes certain cuts of poplar can be whitish, but, by and large, they are more likely to be a yellowish brown and usually have greenish and purplish tinges, which are not realistic colors for animal wildlife.

Always use wood that has been kiln-dried to within 8% moisture content. Avoid wood that has been air-dried as it is likely to shrink and distort when used indoors.

maple. Soft maple cuts easily, takes stains readily, and its sapwood has a beautiful whiteness that, when left unstained, makes excellent natural highlights. Hard sugar maple and those maples with wavy, curly, and even bird's eye figures can also be used but they may be more difficult to cut. In general, avoid boards cut from the heartwood of the maple tree, which is usually a reddish brown in color. The sapwood of nearly all species is light in color and virtually white. Dark woods, such as oak, cherry, walnut, and others are not recommended because they generally lack the natural whiteness necessary for highlighted segments.

Basswood, aspen, birch, balsam fir, spruce, northern white cedar, and certain pines such as western white, sugar, and eastern white pine have creamy to light colors and they generally saw easily. They all, however, accept stains differently and, as a rule, they do not take stains

Many of the projects require wide boards—½" or more in thickness. Generally, it is best to make up wide panels by gluing narrower boards together as shown in Photo No. 1-14. Begin with 1" boards not wider than 4". Presurfaced boards are actually ¾" or ¹³⁄₁₆" thick when purchased. Joint the edges true before gluing. When dry, surface the glued panes on both sides, reducing the overall finished thickness to approximately ½" in thickness. Now you are ready to apply the pattern and begin cutting out the individual segments.

Many of the finished projects are glued to a plywood backer. This is cut slightly smaller all around than the profile outline of the segmented portrait, so it is not visible. Almost any plywood or sheet material ⅛" to ⅜" in thickness can be used for this purpose. Other plaques and framings that are visible components of the project are discussed in Chapter 2 on page 25.

Chapter 2 Basic Techniques

Applying the Pattern

With your wood selected and prepared, you are ready to apply your pattern and begin cutting. Assure that the front surface has been sanded and the dust particles removed with a tack rag. Enlarge the pattern to the desired size, using a photocopy machine. Use scissors to remove the excess paper to within about ½" of the actual pattern. See Photo No. 2-1.

Apply a temporary bonding spray adhesive to the back of the pattern and hand-press the pattern onto the surface of the wood.

Practicing Cuts

For beginners, making some preliminary practice cuts is recommended until confidence is gained and various lines can be followed consistently. Patience and practice are the keys to developing sawing skills.

Beginners should also use the hold-down and guard. Making quick, sharp, "on the spot" turns to cut inside corners and acute angles requires some practice and a fairly narrow blade.

For most projects, the pattern provides thin cutting lines to follow. Try to cut directly on the line. Cutting too far to one side of the line may spoil the integrity of the design.

Some projects require making inside cuts. Simply drill a small hole through the work piece in an inconspicuous place. Thread the blade through the hole in the work piece, reattach it to the saw, and begin cutting.

Photo No. 2-1 A photocopy of the pattern is trimmed with scissors and ready to apply to the wood.

Cutting the Wood

Cut out the pattern segments, using the scroll saw. See Photo No. 1-3 on page 12. Use a medium (No. 5) or smaller (No. 2) blade as dictated by the amount of cutting detail and sharp radius turns required. Remember that all cuts must be perfectly vertical so the cut pieces can separate easily from the uncut segments.

Do not attempt to get extra use from a dull blade. Immediately change to a new blade at the first signs of charring in the cut. This will save you from immense frustration later. Dull blades tend to wander from the line of cut and make inclined cuts that are not vertical. Such poor cutting results in beveled edges that interlock and refuse to separate.

Follow the pattern's cutting lines as closely as possible. Avoid backing up and recutting a line if you happen to wander away from the line of cut. This only widens the saw kerf, which should be maintained as one continuous narrow width or the size of a single cut.

Staining the Pieces

Staining is the second key element of the overall process. See Photo No. 2-2. Staining can be as simple or as complex and artistically challenging as you wish to make it. Protective mess preventative measures are recommended because staining can create quite a muddle. Have wiping rags or paper toweling on hand to clean up spills and drips. Protect work areas with disposable papers, drop cloths, or plastic sheeting. Wear rubber gloves, if having stained hands is offensive, and wear a shop apron to protect clothing.

The staining process is not bound by numerous restraints or "rules." In fact, individualism and experimentation is strongly encouraged. There are, however, a few tips and suggestions that will be helpful. First, when cutting the individual segments free with the scroll saw, mark the back surface of each piece with an "X." This will help to keep the front surfaces properly

Photo No. 2-2 Just two stains, Golden Oak and Dark Walnut, are the primary colors used on every project. Disposable aluminum cake tins are great for dipping and slosh-staining with a foam brush.

oriented when staining and making the subsequent glued assembly. See Photo No. 2-5 on page 23.

Essentially, the staining objective is to use just a few stains or other coloring mediums creatively to achieve a wide range of color tones. Necessary tones should range from deep blacks to levels of medium to a very light brown that still contrasts with the whiteness of the unfinished wood.

Most colors are achieved using just two basic stains. These are Golden Oak and Black or Dark Walnut stains. See Photo No. 2-3. Other stain colors occasionally used for creating highlights and special effects are Red Mahogany and Salem Maple. To achieve a jet black look, simply apply a very heavy coat of Black Walnut stain and wait up to several days for it to dry, or

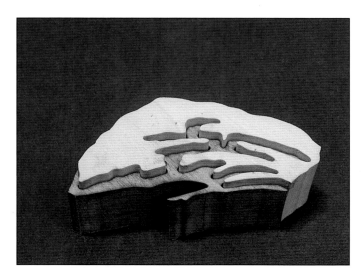

Photo No. 2-3 Notice the color differences between two pieces of soft maple where one is stained Golden Oak and the other is left unstained.

just use a black liquid ink. The color intensity can be controlled somewhat by how the stain is applied and allowed to dry.

By wiping, mixing, combining, and smearing stains together, a near infinite variety and depth of color can be obtained.

When the pattern key specifies "Golden Oak mixed with Black Walnut," this means the two stains are smeared together on the wood, not mixed together in a separate container. Mixing in a pan just creates another even shade. *Note: Generally, unevenness in the application of stain is desirable. Very few things in nature are smooth and perfect; i.e., animal fur is not always groomed—uneven effects look more like natural fur or feathers.*

When two stains are "smear-mixed," this is usually done with one's finger, the corner of a cloth rag, or with a cotton swab. Usually, it is best to smear Dark Walnut stain over the Golden Oak stain while it is still wet. Carefully study project photos. This will help determine which pieces have mixed colors and which do not.

Some lighter tones of Golden Oak stain on areas of certain pieces will also be noticeable. This soft, light-colored effect is accomplished by wiping the surface immediately after the stain has been applied. This technique leaves just a little pigment on the wood—enough to contrast with the unstained pieces. With a little practice with a rag, it is possible to create a blend or faded effect on a highly visible segment. This technique has been effectively applied to the beak on the Intermediate - Eagle Head (front view) on page 72.

Creating a Spotted Look

One method employed on the Intermediate - Fawn on page 80 and the Expert - Leopard on page 99 is to actually cut out the spots or a series of connected spots, stain them separately, and reinsert them. This requires drilling a small blade-threading hole for every cutout. Spotted effects can also be created with contrasting drops or smudges of stain.

The spots on the Leopard are done by first applying a coat of Golden Oak stain and allowing it to partially dry (two to three hours). Then, while it is still "tacky," use a small brush to daub on spots of the same Golden Oak stain.

Since oil and water do not mix, water is another method that can be used to create a spotting effect. Test this first on scrap. Apply the background stain as usual to the wood. While the stain is still wet, drip some water on it and "pat" it around with your finger so you do not have perfectly round drip spots. Once you have manipulated the water to spot or achieve the ruffled fur look you want, allow the piece to dry on a level surface.

Gluing the Assembly

The stained segments are assembled much like the pieces of a puzzle and then glued together. Some of these pieces are positioned higher and elevated above the surfaces of adjoining pieces to create a 3-D relief effect. See Photos No. 2-3 on page 21, No. 2-4, No. 2-5, and No. 2-7 on page 24. The amount of relief can range from $\frac{1}{16}$" to $\frac{3}{16}$"—again there are no hard and fast rules.

The gluing is a very basic process. Simply lay a bead of carpenter's glue over the saw kerf on the back surface. See Photo No. 2-5. Notice that we are not gluing for structural strength, but to maintain the relief level and to keep the pieces sticking to each other. The segments are not glued edge-to-edge as is done in conventional woodworking practices, common segmentation, or intarsia processes. The individual pieces are not glued to a backer either, although some could be. Later, entire portrait assemblies may or may not be glued to a backer, depending entirely on individual choice. Also, there are no

Photo No. 2-4 Here, two adjoining pieces are placed upside-down and positioned for gluing so the unstained piece will be about $\frac{1}{16}$" to $\frac{1}{8}$" in relief on the face side.

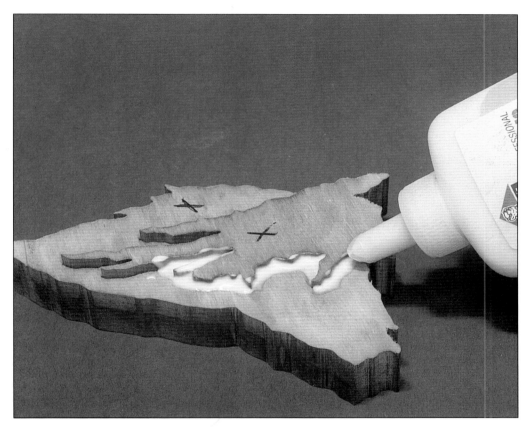

Photo No. 2-5 Run a bead fillet of glue along the saw cuts on the back surface. Notice the "X" marks that indicate the back surfaces.

When viewing real life, the noses of animals and people are the closest to you. Therefore, gluing the nose segment farther out (higher in relief) than the eyes will make the project appear more realistic. Usually, but not always, darker stained pieces are shadows and they are glued farther back. White, unstained pieces represent highlights and these are usually (but not always) glued farther out, closer to the eye of the viewer. Side-by-side segments of the same stained color should alternate up and down slightly to cast small shadows to maintain relief and to give a textured look.

shims glued under elevated segments, as is the practice in basic segmentation and intarsia work.

It may be best to glue separate sections of the portrait together before gluing others. Notice how all of the segments for the head of the Fawn were glued together as a single unit. See Photo No. 2-6 on page 24. The glue tends to run through wide saw kerf openings rather quickly, so turn the work front-side-up as soon as possible to prevent this from happening.

Using Highlighting Techniques

In addition to "smear-mixing" and blending stains to create a realistic look on individual pieces, such as shown in Photo No. 2-6 on page 24, some additional highlighting can be added either before, during, or after gluing the assemblage of segments together. Just a little wipe of Salem Maple stain along one edge can have a dramatic effect. See Photos No. 2-6 through No. 2-9.

Examples of effective use of white paint to represent the glare glistening from a moist nose or to add realism to eyes are shown in Photos No. 2-6, through No. 2-11. Very small dots can be applied with a tooth-pick or the pointed end of a small paintbrush handle.

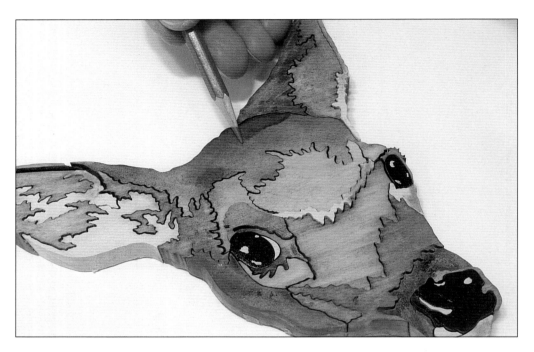

Photo No. 2-6 Here, the piece between the ears has been smear-mixed with the addition of the dark stain over the lighter. Notice the use of just a little red mahogany stain lightly wiped onto the unstained (white) segments in the ears, by the eyes, and just below the nose. Also notice the use of white paint daubed on the eyes and nose.

Photo No. 2-7 Notice the various levels of the glue assembly which create shadows and reduce the prominence of any open saw kerfs. Notice how the white areas of the eye are daubs of white paint applied over the dark stain.

Photo No. 2-8 Here, a little Salem Maple stain was lightly daubed over the Golden Oak to highlight the chin and other areas.

Photo No. 2-9 This close-up shows a little Salem Maple stain above the nose and how just a small dot of white paint on the pupils of the eye brings the character to life.

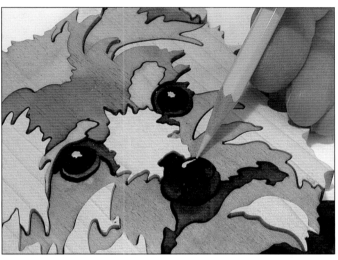

Photo No. 2-11 The painted slash makes the Puppy's nose look moist.

Photo No. 2-10 Notice the eye and nose details.

Using Frames, Plaques, Backers & Display Props

There are numerous ways to display your completed "portrait." One is to frame it with a self-made or purchased molding. See Photo No. 2-12 on page 26. When framing, the portrait can be glued to a natural plywood backer that is unfinished, or whatever is desired. Usually, it is best to omit the placement of glass when framing.

Various simple plaques with routed edges, such as were developed for the Intermediate - Vertical Flying Eagle on page 64 and the Intermediate - Black Bear on page 84, are other alternatives. Notice the rustic log slab plaque for the mounting of the Eagle Head (front view). See Photo No. 2-16 on page 28.

Photo No. 2-12 The Fawn portrait is framed without glass.

Photo No. 2-13 Some projects look great without any sort of fabricated background or plaque.

Many of the projects are nicely displayed without any kind of visible plaque or backer. In such cases, it is best to cut a backer from a piece of ⅛"- or ¼"-thick plywood slightly smaller (⅛" to ¼") all around the profile outline of the portrait. Then glue the portrait to the backer, using construction-type gap-filling mastic or silicone adhesive. This adds to the structural integrity of the project without any visual distraction. The Staring Wolf and Big Horn Ram are shown without backing plaques. See Photos No. 2-13 and No. 2-14. The Big Horn Ram is also shown mounted to a simple painted plywood backer and a novel simulated stone plaque. See Photos No. 2-15 and No. 2-17 on page 28.

Photo No. 2-14 Here, the Big Horn Ram portrait is finished without a visible backer.

Photo No. 2-15 Here, the Big Horn Ram is finished with a simple, painted plywood plaque backer.

Photo No. 2-16 The Eagle Head (front view) is mounted on a rustic slab plaque.

Making Simulated Stone Plaques

The simulated stone backer shown in Photo No. 2-17 is a complementary way to mount wildlife portraits. A piece of ½"-thick exterior plywood covered with ¼" wire mesh provides the foundation for applying a home-use concrete

Photo No. 2-17 Here, the Big Horn Ram is mounted on a simulated stone backer.

patching mix. Cut the desired shape from the plywood and attach the wire mesh with a staple gun. Fold the edges over and attach to the back. See Photos No. 2-18, through No. 2-20.

Home-use concrete patching mix is available at local hardware stores and mixes with water. Wear rubber gloves and hand-smear the mixed patching compound onto the backer board.

While the mixture is still soft, stipple the surface with the bristle ends of a whisk broom to create a realistic-looking stone texture. When dry, attach the assembled wood portrait to the front surface with silicone, epoxy, or structural adhesive.

Unusual rustic- or rugged-looking pieces of wood burls or even real stones and the like make interesting props to include in a free-standing arrangement. See the Expert - White-tailed Deer on page 89, the Standing Ram on page 110, and the Cougar on page 112. All are good examples of ways to create natural-looking props or surroundings to display your wildlife portrait sculptures.

Photo No. 2-19 Attach ¼" wire mesh to the plywood to serve as a reinforcement for the patching compound. Flatten the folded wire mesh to create natural-looking, irregular edges.

Photo No. 2-18 Cut a rough shape from inexpensive CD-grade plywood to make a simulated stone background plaque.

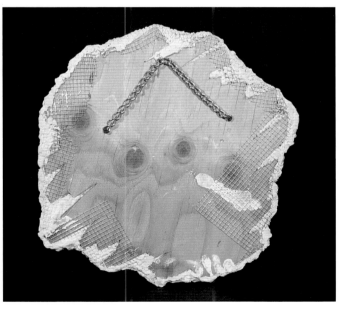

Photo No. 2-20 This rear view shows the heavy hanging chain and the edges of patching compound attached to the plywood with the "wrap" of wire mesh.

Chapter 3

Beginner - Sailboat

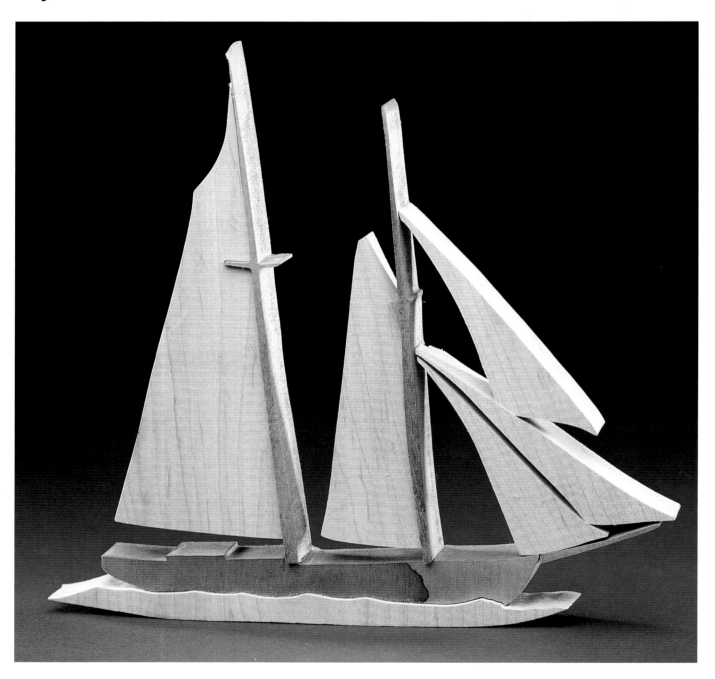

The Beginner - Sailboat was designed to be an easy piece to give
you practice cutting. This project is 7" tall and has only 10 pieces.

BEGINNER - SAILBOAT PATTERN

Enlarge pattern 153%

☐ No Stain

☐ Golden Oak

■ Golden Oak mixed with
Black Walnut

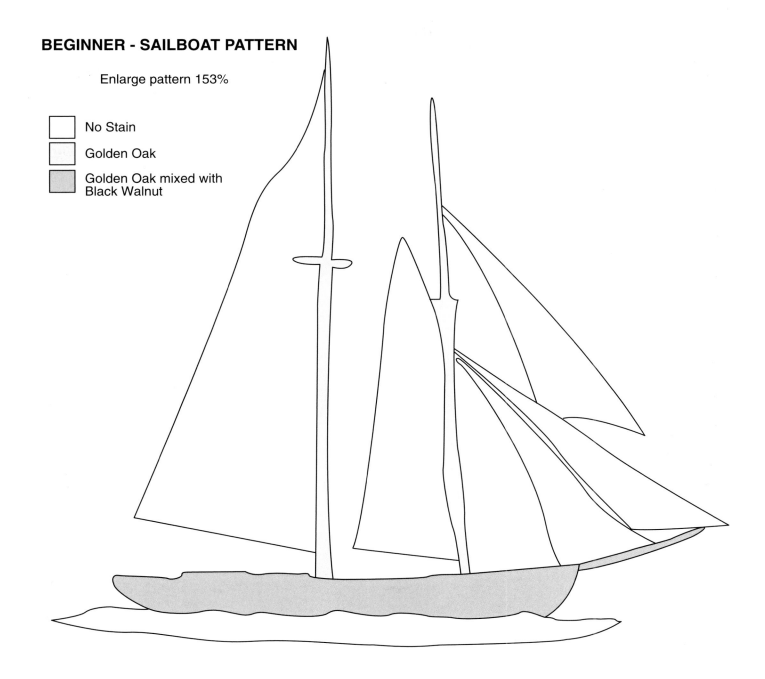

Beginner - Airplane

This airplane is a nice beginner piece to start with. It measures 10¼" long and 3½" tall. It isn't very big. There are only 30 pieces, so it can be a leisurely afternoon project.

Start with the top wing first. Cut the braces of the wings, then the propeller, body of the airplane, lower wings, and finally the wheels.

Stain the tires with a black liquid ink. Leave the struts on the wheels natural unstained maple so they stand out better. Stain the back wheel support golden oak. Color the little wheel with black liquid ink.

Stain the body with golden oak mixed with black walnut. Stain it golden oak first, then dip a finger in the black walnut and smear it lightly on so it is a darker brown than the golden oak alone gives.

Stain the engine black walnut, without wiping it off. (Some stains I apply and then wipe off immediately so they are not so dark.) Stain the propeller natural unstained maple. Stain the top wing golden oak, and leave the supports a natural unstained maple. Stain the lower wing dark walnut, leaving a strip across the top of it natural unstained maple. The tail piece is also left natural unstained maple.

BEGINNER - AIRPLANE PATTERN

Enlarge pattern 105%

No Stain

Golden Oak

Black Walnut (wiped off)

Black Walnut (heavy)

33

Beginner - Howling Wolf

This project is approximately 10" tall and has only 24 pieces.
He looks terrific on an oval backer after he is finished.

BEGINNER - HOWLING WOLF PATTERN

Enlarge pattern 125%

Paint white dot on eye.
Refer to photograph
for placement.

No Stain

Golden Oak

Golden Oak mixed with Black Walnut

Black Walnut (heavy)

Beginner - Eagle Head (side view)

Here is a simple way to begin your odyssey of cutting realistic-looking eagles.
This eagle is approximately 6" square and is made up of just 16 pieces.

BEGINNER - EAGLE HEAD (side view)
PATTERN

Enlarge pattern 117%

No Stain

Golden Oak

Golden Oak mixed with Black Walnut

Black Walnut (heavy)

Paint white dot on eye.
Refer to photograph
for placement.

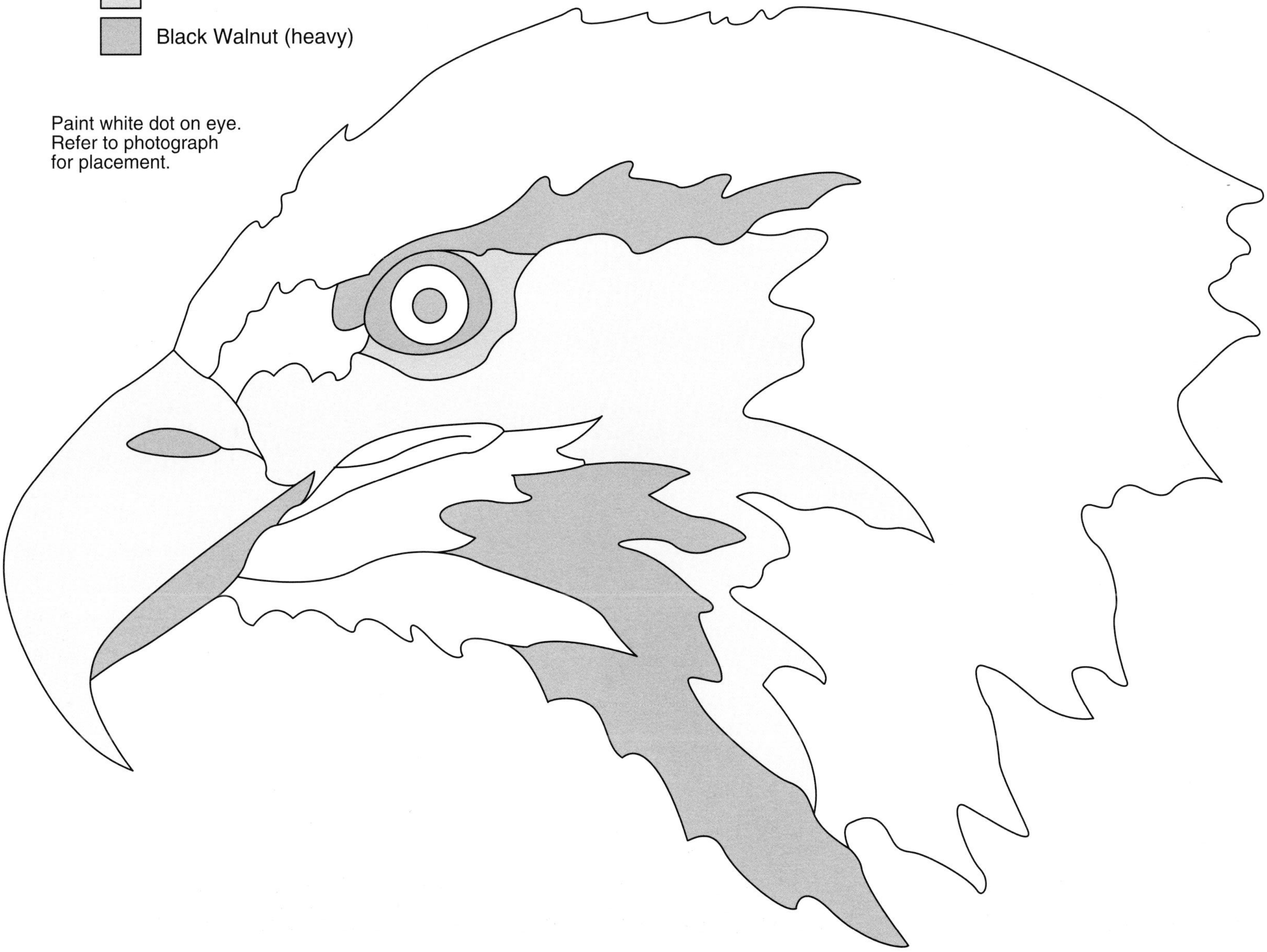

Beginner - Songbird

This little fellow is a favorite. He is made up of 21 pieces. If desired, you can make him larger or smaller. The enlargement recommended on the pattern is for a 10" model. This songbird is quite a fun and simple pattern to cut out.

Begin by cutting the beak and then the eye and pupil. Continue to the neck and the crown of the head. The body is next and then the three sections of the wing. Move to the legs and the twig, and end by moving down from the top of the tail feathers.

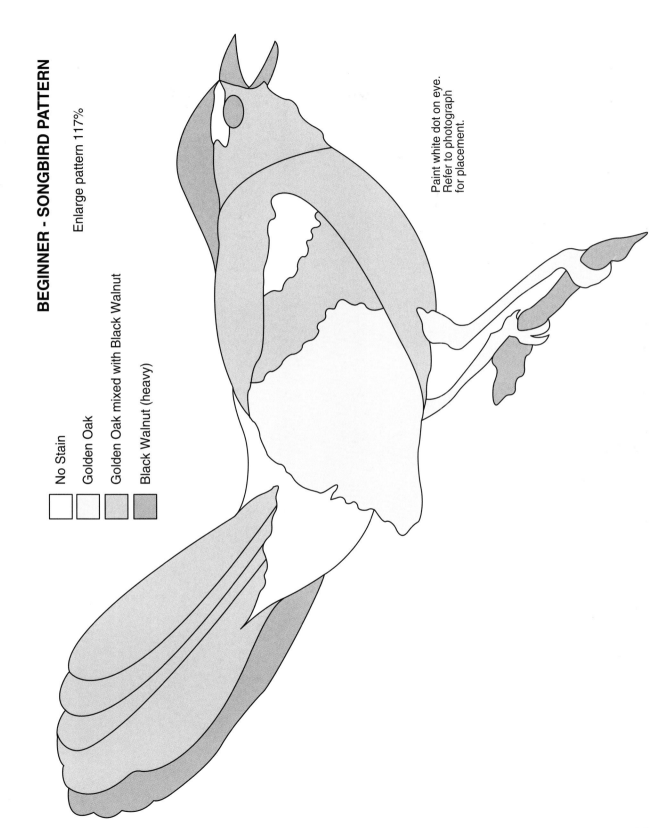

BEGINNER - SONGBIRD PATTERN

Enlarge pattern 117%

No Stain

Golden Oak

Golden Oak mixed with Black Walnut

Black Walnut (heavy)

Paint white dot on eye.
Refer to photograph
for placement.

39

Beginner - Kingfisher

This saucy little guy is one of the easiest patterns to cut. The finished project stands approximately 8" tall. He is a mere 20 pieces.

BEGINNER - KINGFISHER PATTERN

Enlarge pattern 111%

Paint white dot on eye.
Refer to photograph
for placement.

No Stain

Golden Oak

Black Walnut (wiped off)

Golden Oak mixed with Black Walnut

Black Walnut (heavy)

41

What a priceless expression! I get laughs from everyone who sees this little guy. He is cut from an 8" square of wood and is made up of 31 pieces.

BEGINNER - CHIMP PATTERN

Enlarge pattern 143%

☐ No Stain

☐ Golden Oak

▨ Golden Oak mixed with Black Walnut

▨ Black Walnut (heavy)

Paint white dots on eyes.
Refer to photograph
for placement.

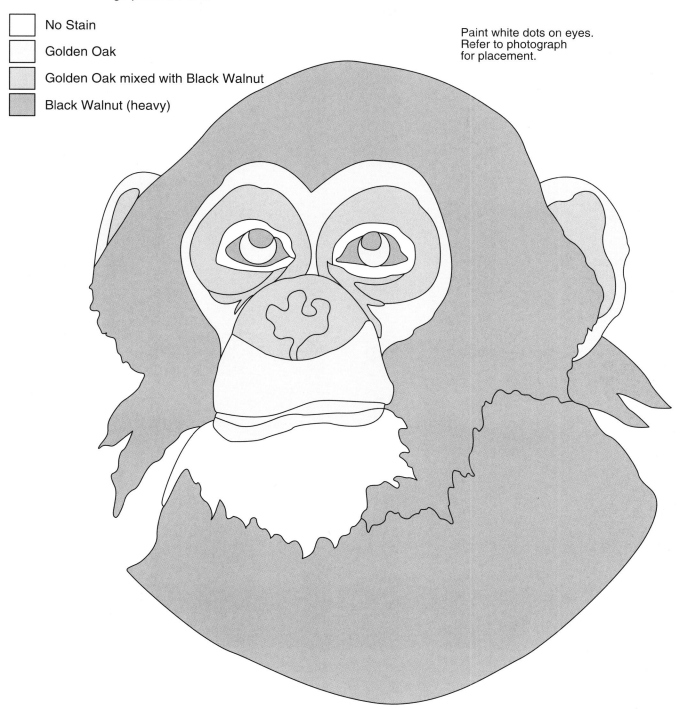

Beginner - Lighthouse Scene

People and animals are not the only things you can cut as portraits. This lighthouse is a delightful change of pace.

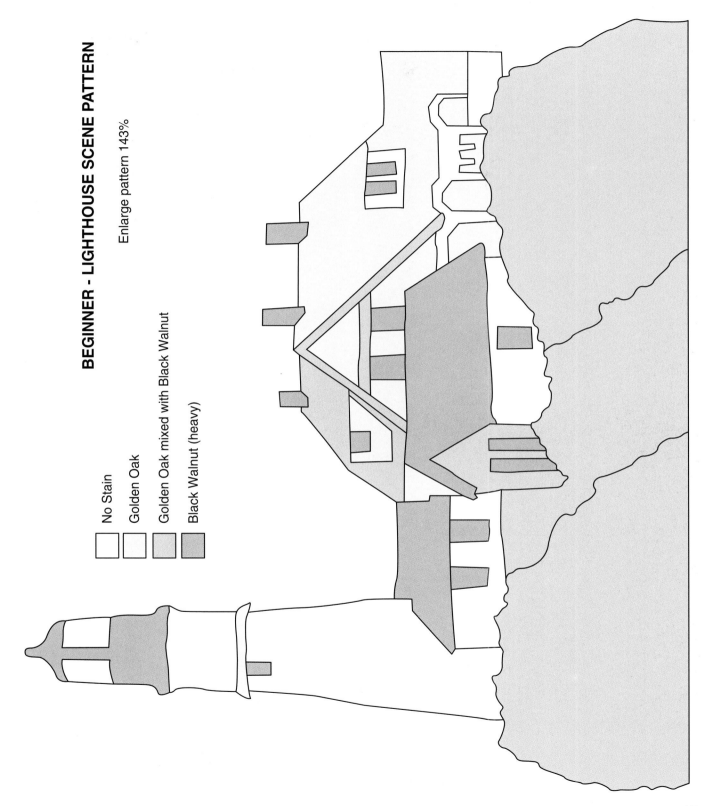

BEGINNER - LIGHTHOUSE SCENE PATTERN

Enlarge pattern 143%

No Stain

Golden Oak

Golden Oak mixed with Black Walnut

Black Walnut (heavy)

45

Beginner - Kitty Cat

Here, we begin with a simple kitty before moving on to more amazing cats. This one is approximately 8" square and is made up of 29 pieces.

BEGINNER - KITTY CAT PATTERN

Enlarge pattern 167%

☐ No Stain

☐ Golden Oak

▨ Golden Oak mixed with Black Walnut

▨ Black Walnut (heavy)

Paint white dots on eyes.
Refer to photograph
for placement.

Beginner - Puppy

Is this the cutest little fellow you've ever seen? He is only 5" square, but you can make him larger if you wish. He has only 24 pieces.

BEGINNER - PUPPY PATTERN

Enlarge pattern 134%

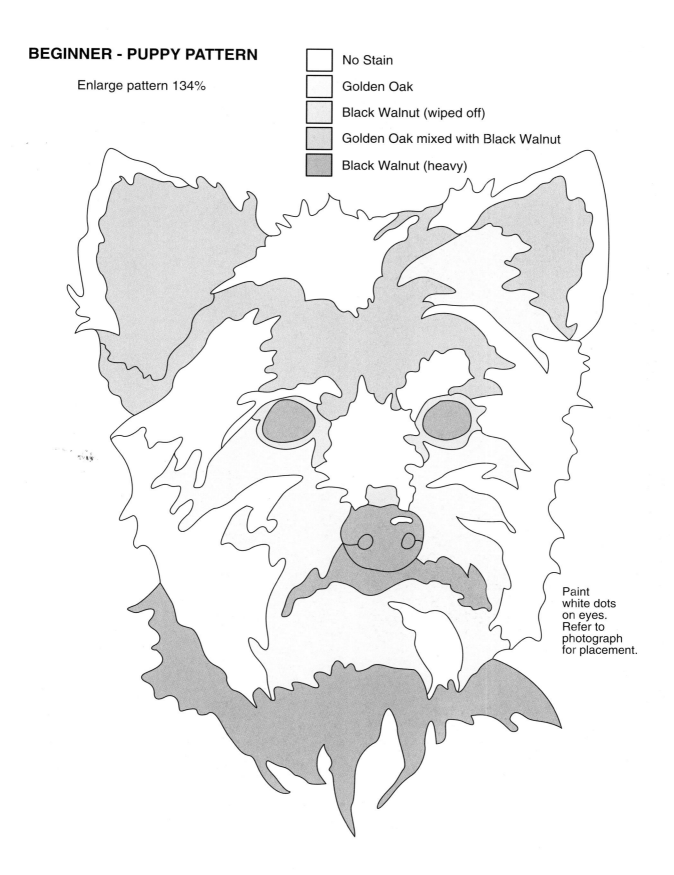

No Stain

Golden Oak

Black Walnut (wiped off)

Golden Oak mixed with Black Walnut

Black Walnut (heavy)

Paint
white dots
on eyes.
Refer to
photograph
for placement.

Isn't he a beauty? This finished project is approximately 10" tall. He is made up of only 35 pieces.

BEGINNER - STARING WOLF PATTERN

Enlarge pattern 143%

Paint white dots on eyes.
Refer to photograph
for placement.

No Stain

Golden Oak

Black Walnut (wiped off)

Black Walnut (heavy)

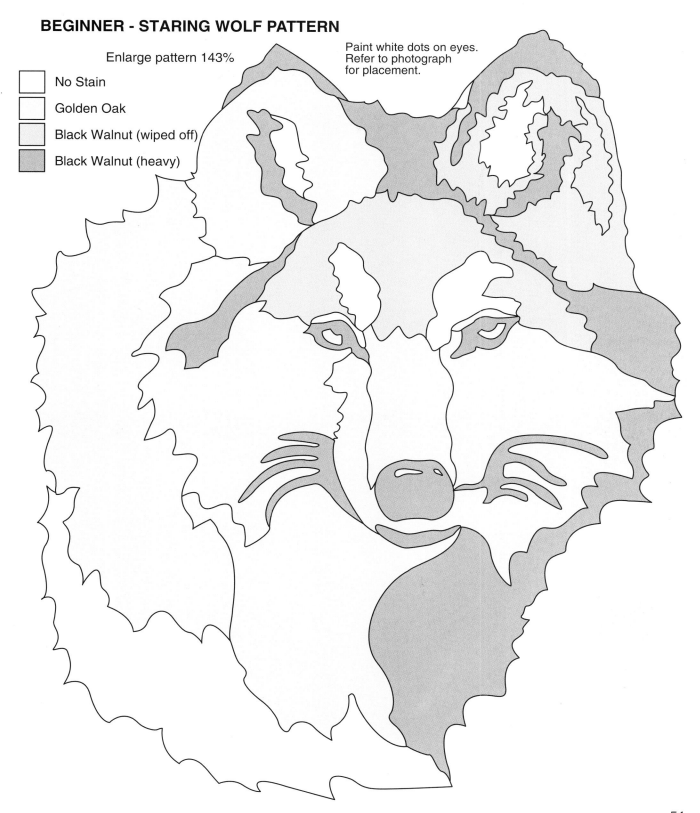

51

Beginner - Bear Head

BEGINNER - BEAR HEAD PATTERN

Actual size pattern

No Stain

Black Walnut (wiped off)

Golden Oak mixed with Black Walnut

Black Walnut (heavy)

Paint white dots on eyes.
Refer to photograph
for placement.

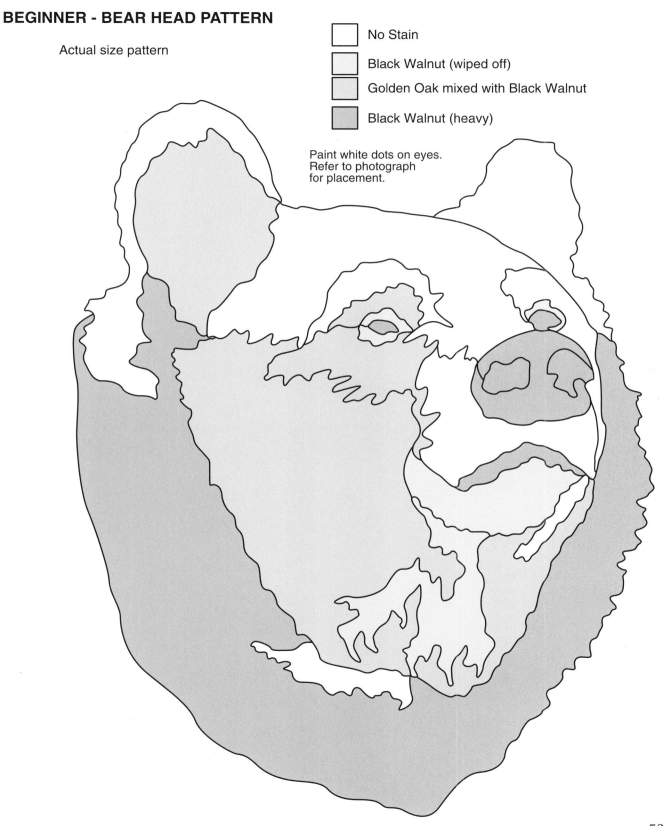

BEGINNER - FISH PATTERN

Actual size pattern

☐ No Stain

☐ Golden Oak

☐ Black Walnut (wiped off)

☐ Golden Oak mixed with Black Walnut

Paint white dot on eye.
Refer to photograph
for placement.

Beginner - Big Horn Ram

With this piece you receive a bonus, not only is a beginner pattern provided, but also an intermediate and an advanced pattern.

This beginner project is made up of only 30 pieces, making for a wonderful way to spend an afternoon.

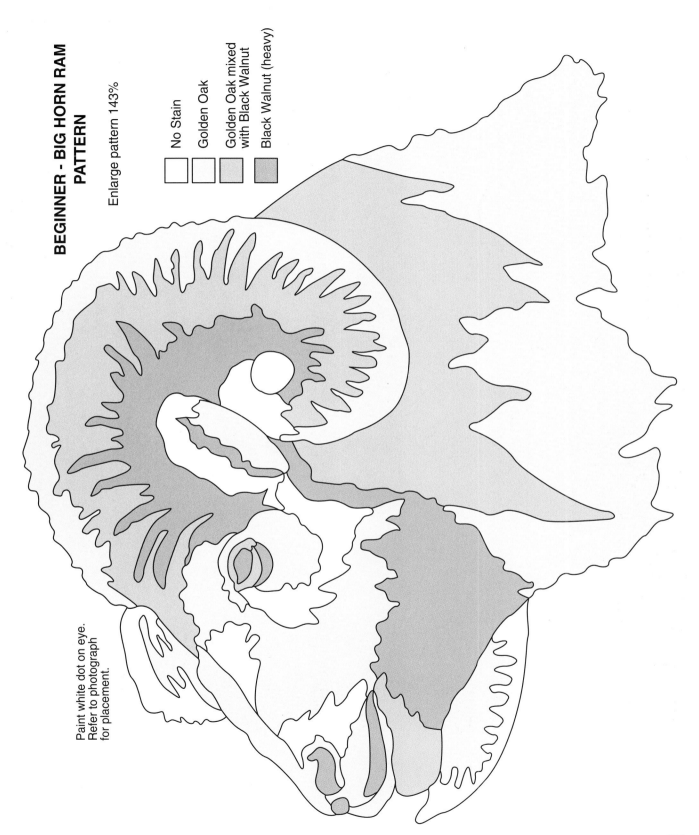

BEGINNER - BIG HORN RAM PATTERN

Enlarge pattern 143%

No Stain

Golden Oak

Golden Oak mixed
with Black Walnut

Black Walnut (heavy)

Paint white dot on eye.
Refer to photograph
for placement.

Beginner - Zebra

This is simply one of the most unique creatures on earth. Cutting one out will help you appreciate the beauty of these incredible animals. This project is approximately 7" tall, but can be cut larger if you prefer. He has 70 pieces. Believe it or not, the Zebra is really quite easy to cut as he is mostly made up of stripes!

BEGINNER - ZEBRA PATTERN

Enlarge pattern 117%

No Stain

Golden Oak

Golden Oak mixed
with Black Walnut

Black Walnut (heavy)

Paint white dot
on eye.
Refer to
photograph
for placement.

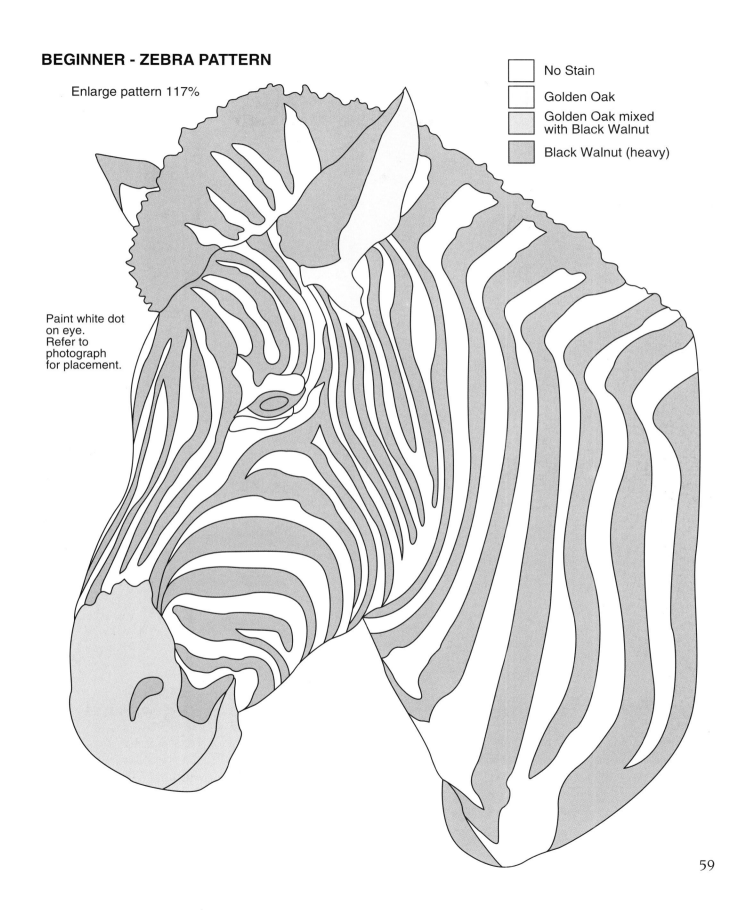

59

Beginner - Sable

Here, the majestic horns of the sable make a perfect practice project. The finished project is approximately 9" tall. You can cut him 12"–15" tall and he'll look terrific! He has a few more pieces than the previous projects, 70 pieces in all. The Beginner - Sable is a simple project.

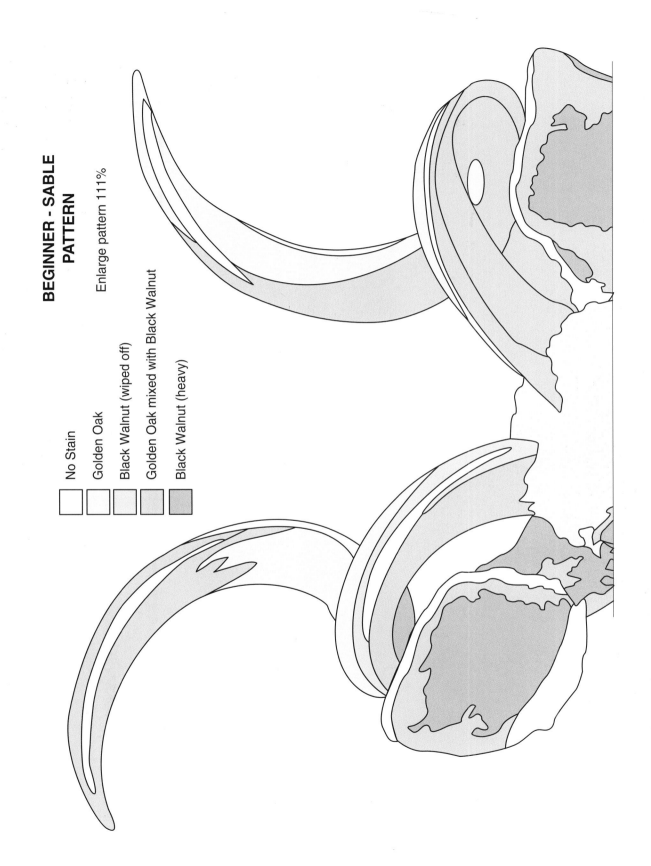

BEGINNER - SABLE PATTERN

Enlarge pattern 111%

No Stain
Golden Oak
Black Walnut (wiped off)
Golden Oak mixed with Black Walnut
Black Walnut (heavy)

61

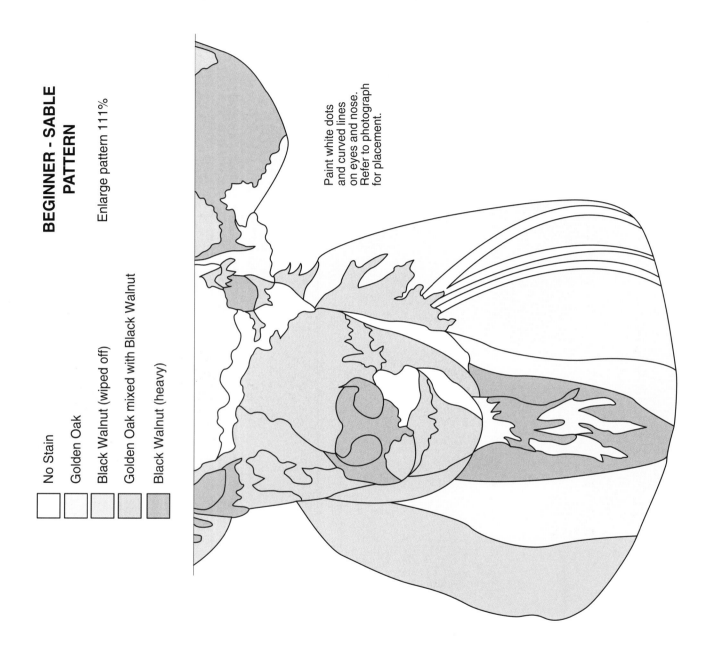

BEGINNER - SABLE PATTERN

Enlarge pattern 111%

Paint white dots and curved lines on eyes and nose. Refer to photograph for placement.

- No Stain
- Golden Oak
- Black Walnut (wiped off)
- Golden Oak mixed with Black Walnut
- Black Walnut (heavy)

Beginner - Penguin

This little guy is enough to melt anyone's heart. He has only 10 pieces and goes together quite quickly. There is a good portion of his stomach that does not need to be stained which further simplifies this pattern. The maple wood makes a perfect contrast to the heavy dark walnut stain used for the back and the head. He can be enlarged for a more life-sized creation.

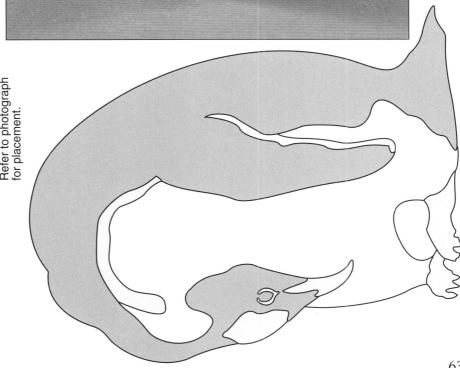

BEGINNER - PENGUIN PATTERN

Enlarge pattern 125%

Paint white dot on eye.
Refer to photograph
for placement.

No Stain

Golden Oak

Black Walnut (heavy)

63

Chapter 4

Intermediate - Vertical Flying Eagle

The only real difference between intermediate projects and beginner projects is that the intermediate projects have more pieces, and hence look more realistic. These projects take a little longer to cut, as well as stain and glue. However, the rewards are simply delightful. To see my friends' and family members' mouths drop and to hear them tell me "I've never seen anything like it!" are what keep me going in scroll sawing.

Here is another eagle that is quite fun to cut. This one is 21" tall. However, I have cut these as large as 36" tall. Eagles are always well liked.

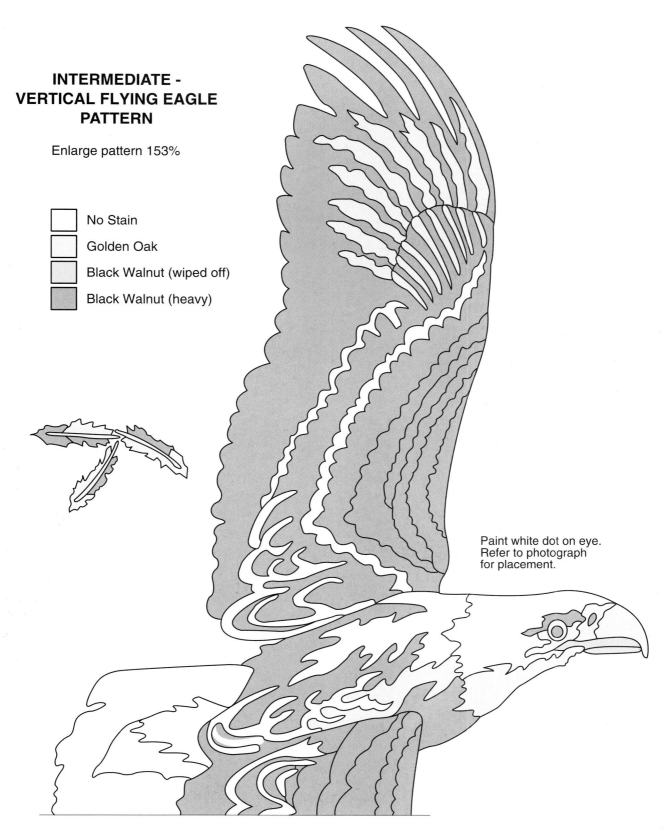

INTERMEDIATE -
VERTICAL FLYING EAGLE
PATTERN

Enlarge pattern 153%

No Stain

Golden Oak

Black Walnut (wiped off)

Black Walnut (heavy)

Paint white dot on eye.
Refer to photograph
for placement.

INTERMEDIATE - VERTICAL FLYING EAGLE PATTERN

Enlarge pattern 153%

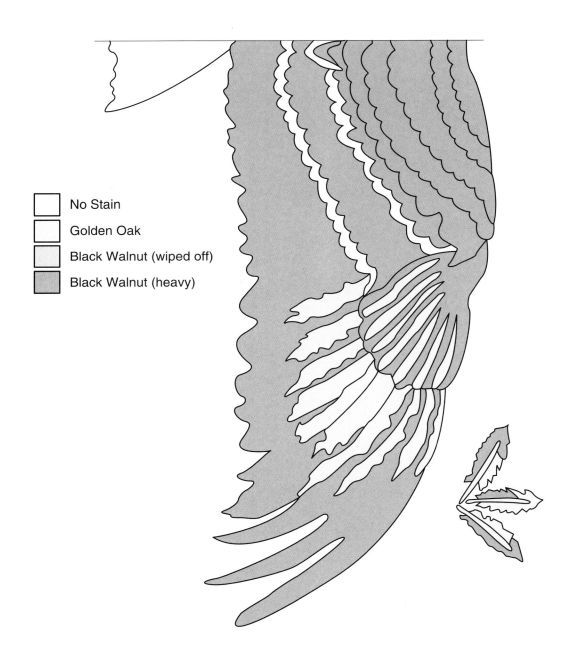

No Stain

Golden Oak

Black Walnut (wiped off)

Black Walnut (heavy)

Intermediate - Bugling Elk with Cows

This is one of the projects I cut and donate to the NRA (National Rifle Association) annual local auction. I do a different animal every year. Another more enjoyable aspect of cutting art pieces is that you can actually do something you love as well as being able to help your favorite charities.

I enjoy this project for another reason—it is more of a scene rather than a single animal head. This helps promote the concept of art,

not just a craft project. The finished, framed project measures 31" x 23".

Start by cutting the grass clumps. Work up the legs and around to the main part of the body. Cut the neck starting with the dark underside piece. This leads you to the head. Next, cut out the mouth, move to the nose and then the eye and ear. Finally the antlers are cut. Cut one elk at a time and then move on to another one. The geese are cut last. Clouds are optional, pattern not included.

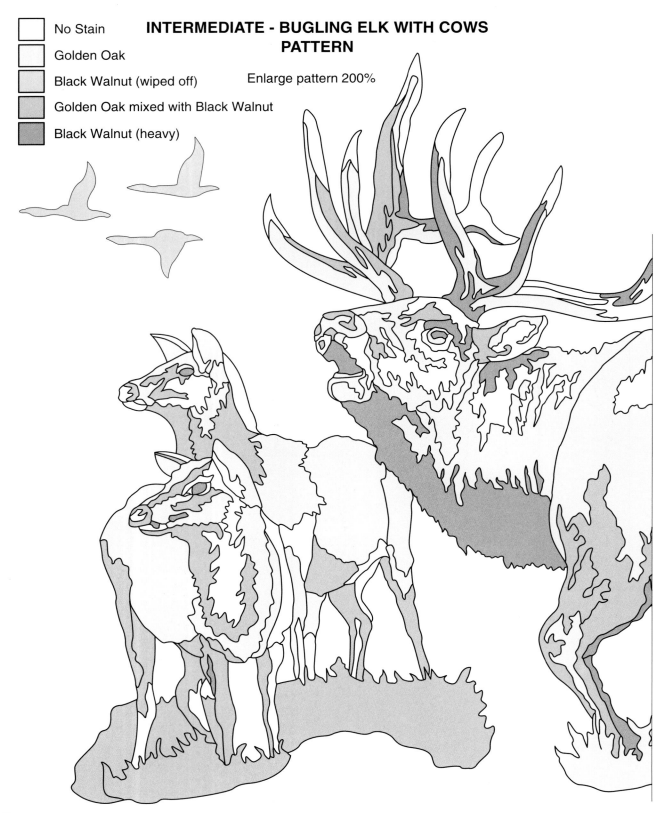

No Stain

Golden Oak

Black Walnut (wiped off)

Golden Oak mixed with Black Walnut

Black Walnut (heavy)

INTERMEDIATE - BUGLING ELK WITH COWS PATTERN

Enlarge pattern 200%

INTERMEDIATE - BUGLING ELK WITH COWS PATTERN

Enlarge pattern 200%

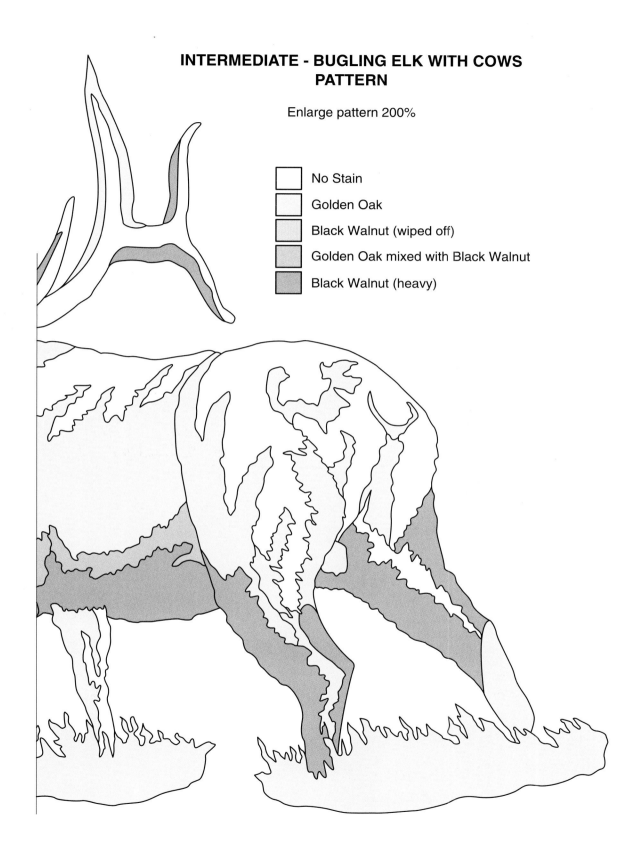

- No Stain
- Golden Oak
- Black Walnut (wiped off)
- Golden Oak mixed with Black Walnut
- Black Walnut (heavy)

Intermediate - Duck

Wood ducks have a lot of detail in them to show off. The actual size of this pattern is only 8" long, but you can cut him longer and larger.

INTERMEDIATE - DUCK PATTERN

Enlarge pattern 117%

No Stain

Golden Oak

Golden Oak mixed with Black Walnut

Red Mahogany

Black Walnut (heavy)

Paint white dot on eye.
Refer to photograph
for placement.

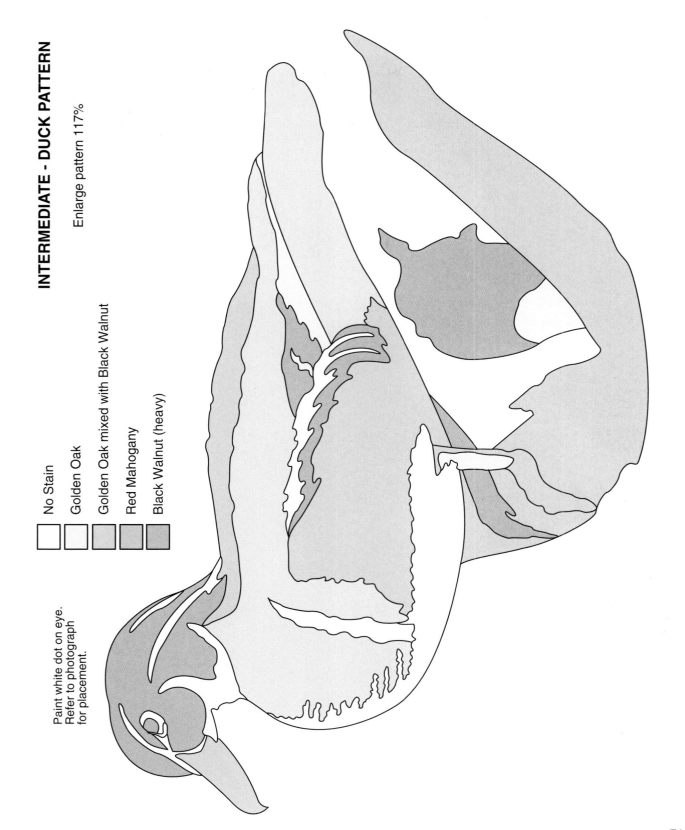

Intermediate - Eagle Head (front view)

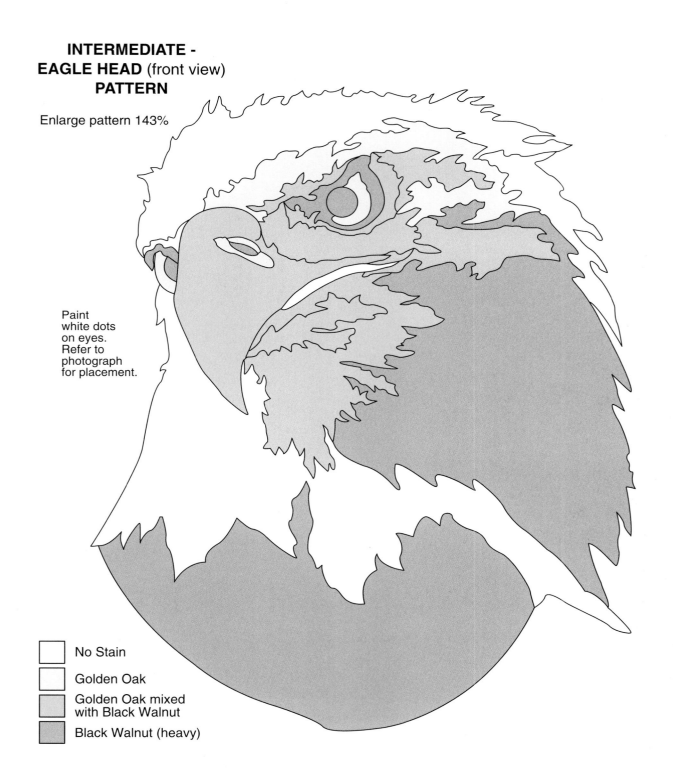

**INTERMEDIATE -
EAGLE HEAD** (front view)
PATTERN

Enlarge pattern 143%

Paint
white dots
on eyes.
Refer to
photograph
for placement.

No Stain

Golden Oak

Golden Oak mixed
with Black Walnut

Black Walnut (heavy)

Intermediate - Big Horn Ram

More detailed pieces can be offset-glued quite prominently. While this makes them look a little odd from a real close view, they start popping into 3-D as you step back. Think of the project as an actual animal, person, or thing (whichever you are cutting as you glue it together. In this instance, the big curly horn is closest to you, so glue it farthest out. His other horn is behind his chin and neck and curls behind his head, so you glue it farther back as if it really is going behind. If an animal is looking directly at you, then glue the nose farthest out.

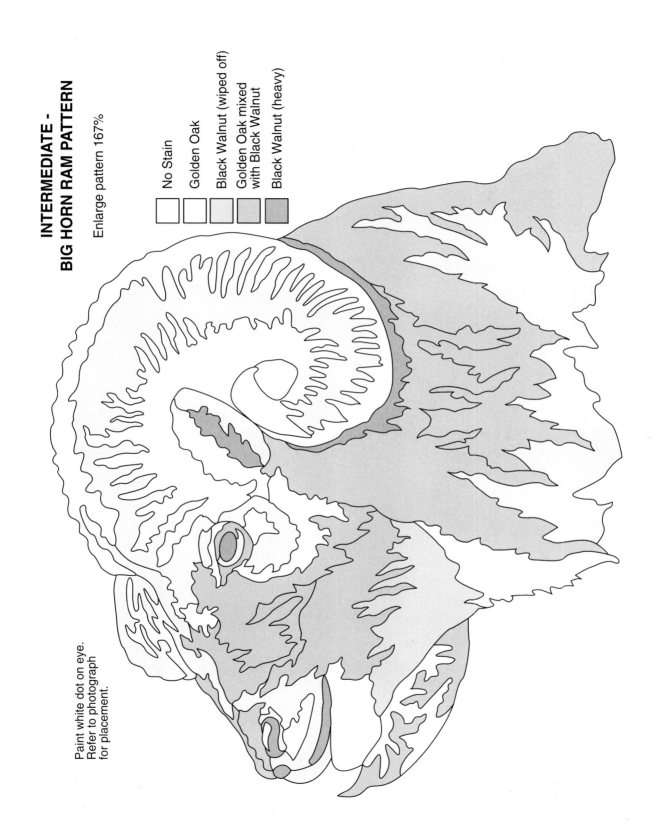

INTERMEDIATE - BIG HORN RAM PATTERN

Enlarge pattern 167%

- No Stain
- Golden Oak
- Black Walnut (wiped off)
- Golden Oak mixed with Black Walnut
- Black Walnut (heavy)

Paint white dot on eye. Refer to photograph for placement.

INTERMEDIATE - STARING WOLF PATTERN

Enlarge pattern 111%

☐ No Stain

☐ Golden Oak

Golden Oak mixed
with Black Walnut

Black Walnut (heavy)

Paint white dots on eyes.
Refer to photograph
for placement.

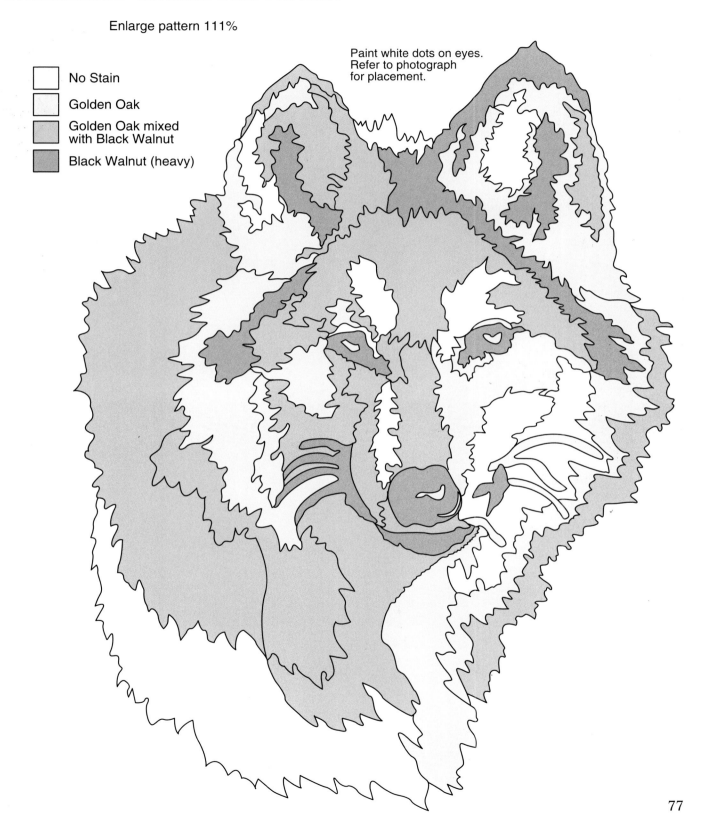

Intermediate - Lion Head

This piece is cut out with a No. 2 scroll saw blade. Excellent detail can result from using this blade and being very patient. It is best to go about half speed with this blade, causing less breakage. Glue the lion's lower body back farthest, with his mane flaring out. The white chin is closest to you, so it is glued the farthest out.

INTERMEDIATE - LION HEAD PATTERN

Enlarge pattern 167%

- No Stain
- Golden Oak
- Black Walnut (wiped off)
- Golden Oak mixed with Black Walnut
- Black Walnut (heavy)

Paint
white dots
on eyes.
Refer to
photograph
for placement.

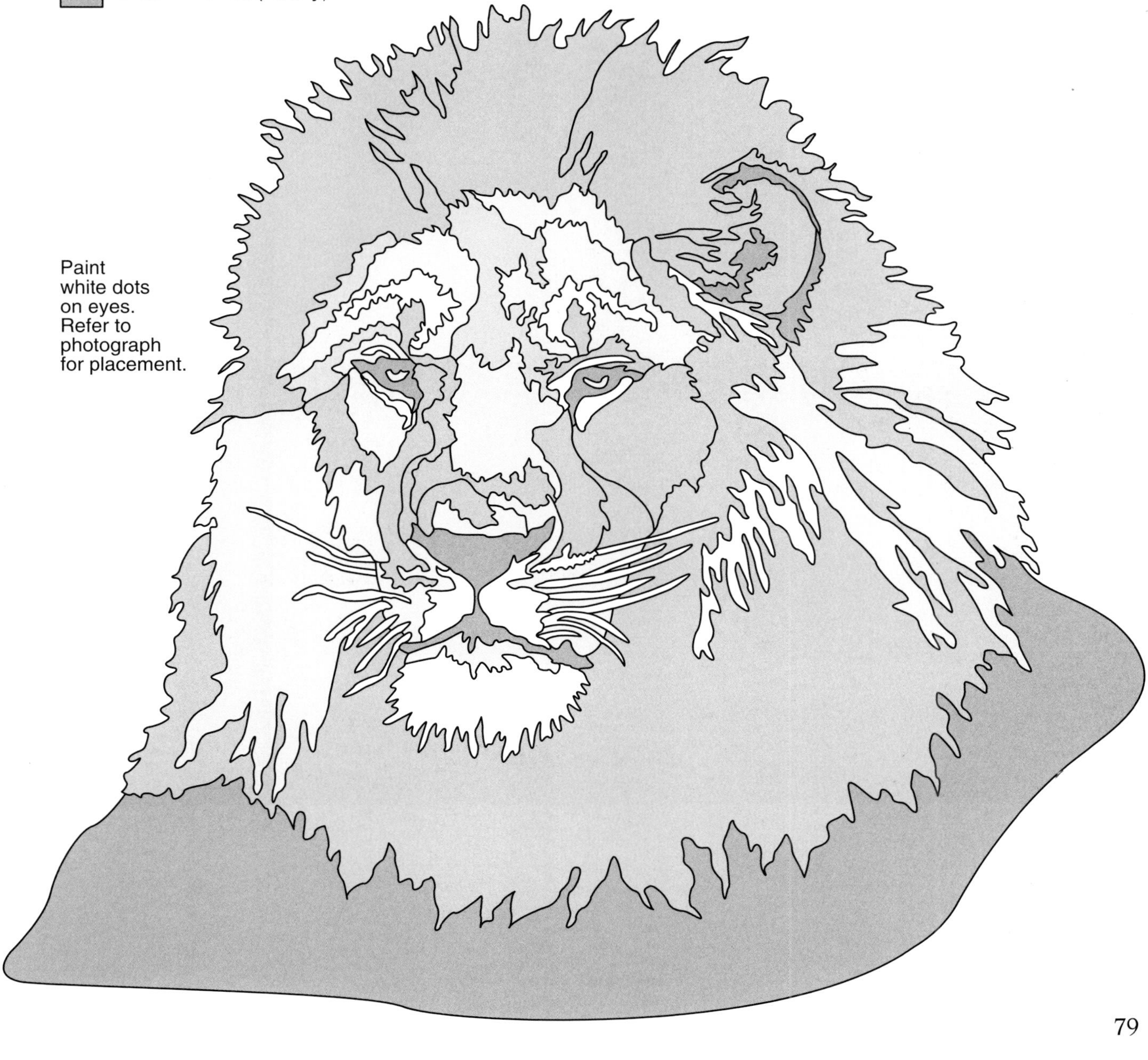

79

Intermediate - Fawn

This particular piece is one where we have to predrill blade entry holes before cutting the spots. Otherwise, simple sawing is used throughout. The exciting thing about this project is the opportunity to combine scrolling techniques to develop a piece of art. Never be afraid to experiment. The fun is in trying new techniques to make a unique piece of art for yourself or others, no two are ever the same. This framed project measures 17½" by 16¼".

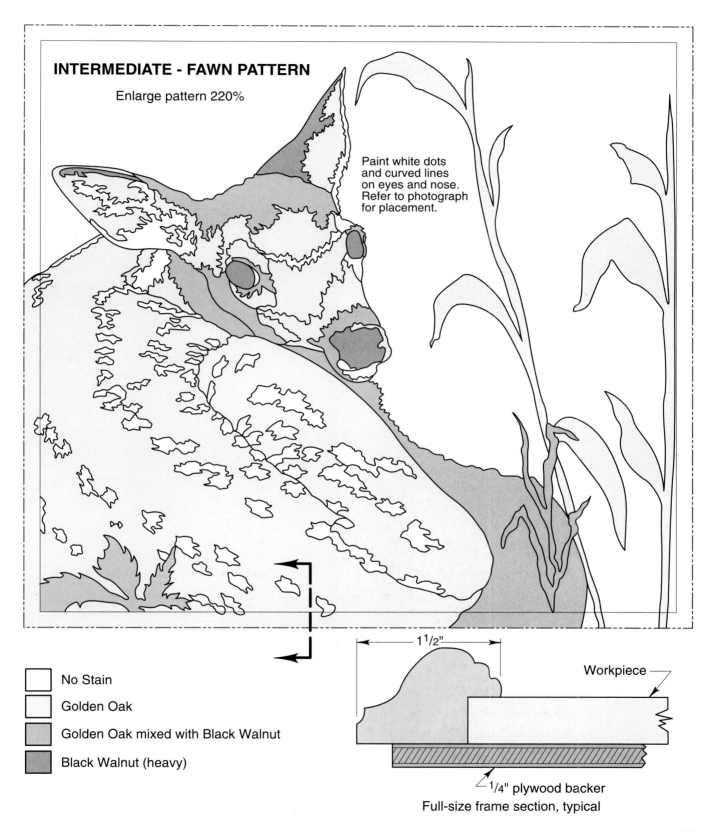

INTERMEDIATE - FAWN PATTERN

Enlarge pattern 220%

Paint white dots
and curved lines
on eyes and nose.
Refer to photograph
for placement.

No Stain

Golden Oak

Golden Oak mixed with Black Walnut

Black Walnut (heavy)

1¹/₂"

Workpiece

¹/₄" plywood backer

Full-size frame section, typical

Intermediate - The "Duke"

KERRY A. SHIRTS 1999

It is rewarding to capture people in wood. Use a No. 2 scroll saw blade to cut out the eyes. Using this blade here can make the piece look like the actual person. If you can capture the essence of their eyes, you can capture their essence entirely.

INTERMEDIATE - THE "DUKE"
PATTERN

Actual size pattern

☐ No Stain

☐ Golden Oak

☐ Black Walnut (wiped off)

☐ Golden Oak mixed with Black Walnut

☐ Red Mahogany

☐ Black Walnut (heavy)

Paint white dots on eyes. Refer to photograph for placement.

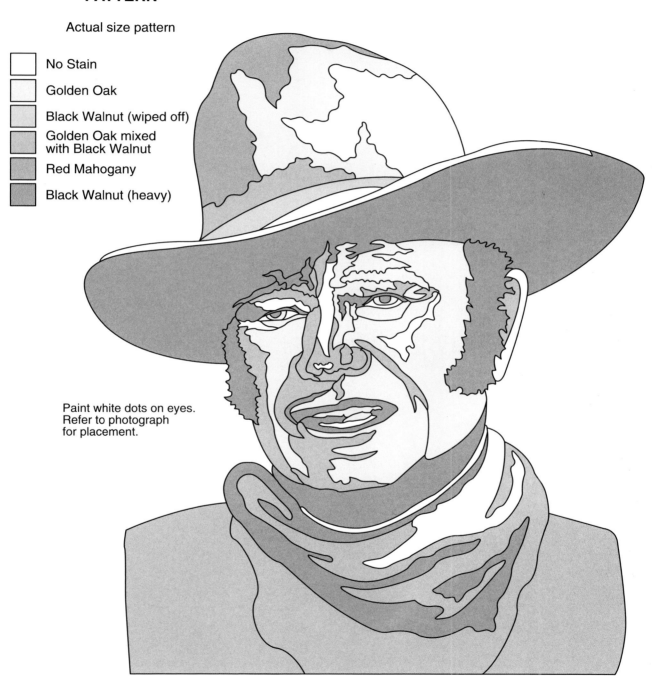

Intermediate - Black Bear

INTERMEDIATE - BLACK BEAR PATTERN

No Stain

Golden Oak

Golden Oak mixed
with Black Walnut

Black Walnut (heavy)

Enlarge pattern 143%

Paint white dots on eyes.
Refer to photograph
for placement.

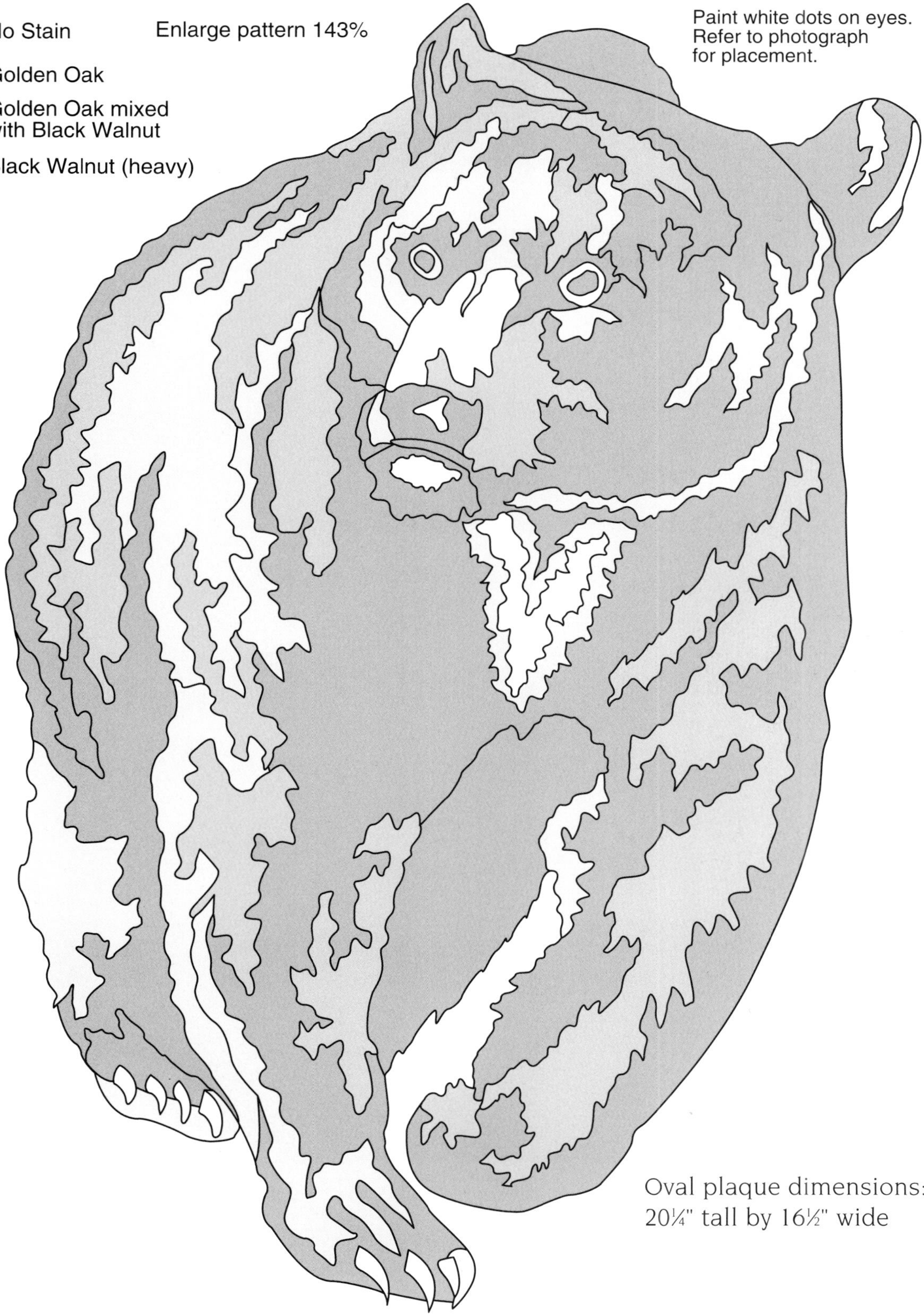

Oval plaque dimensions:
20¼" tall by 16½" wide

Expert - Big Horn Ram

This is the same Big Horn Ram used for Beginner and Intermediate projects, but this one has more pieces. It is approximately 10" square and mounted on a simulated stone plaque. The curly maple used actually adds to its dimensionality.

EXPERT - BIG HORN RAM PATTERN

Enlarge pattern 167%

- No Stain
- Golden Oak
- Golden Oak mixed with Black Walnut
- Black Walnut (heavy)

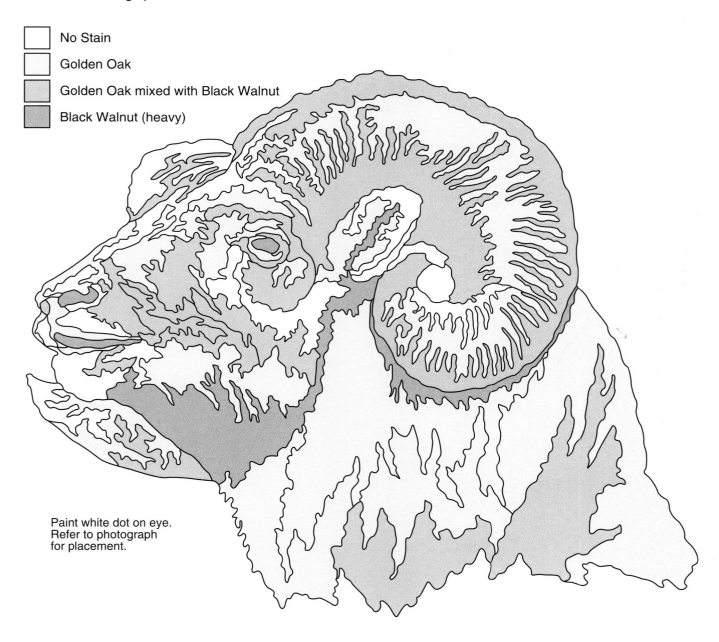

Paint white dot on eye.
Refer to photograph
for placement.

EXPERT - BIG HORN RAM PLAQUE PATTERN

Enlarge pattern 286%

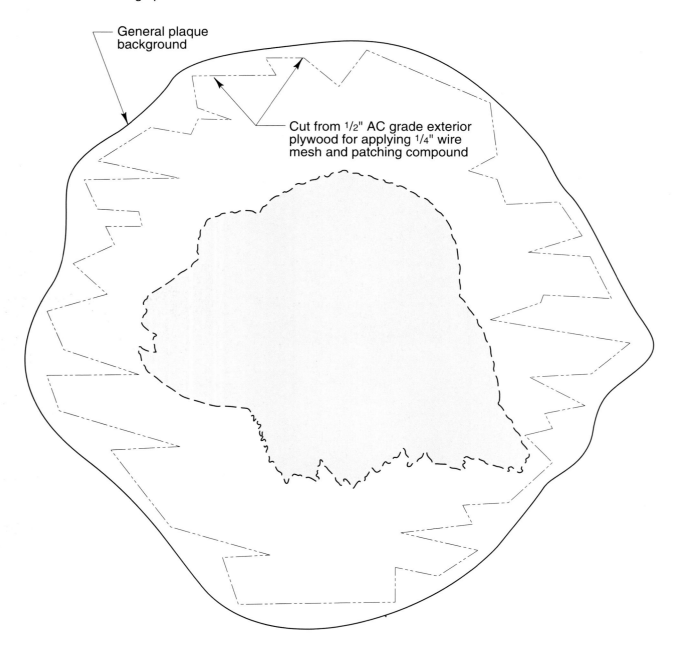

General plaque background

Cut from 1/2" AC grade exterior plywood for applying 1/4" wire mesh and patching compound

EXPERT - WHITE-TAILED DEER PATTERN

Enlarge pattern 167%

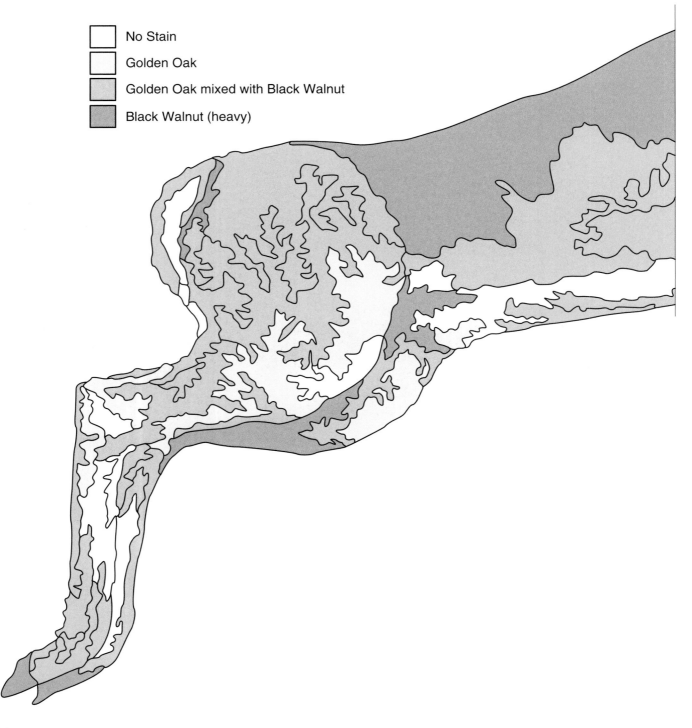

- ☐ No Stain
- ☐ Golden Oak
- ▨ Golden Oak mixed with Black Walnut
- ▧ Black Walnut (heavy)

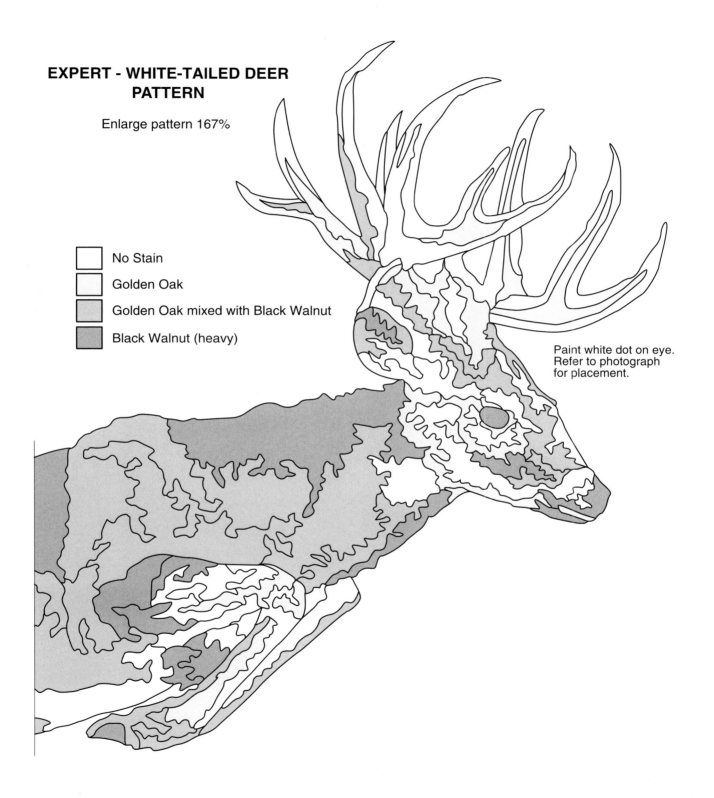

EXPERT - WHITE-TAILED DEER PATTERN

Enlarge pattern 167%

- No Stain
- Golden Oak
- Golden Oak mixed with Black Walnut
- Black Walnut (heavy)

Paint white dot on eye.
Refer to photograph
for placement.

EXPERT - CUSTER PATTERN

Enlarge pattern 200%

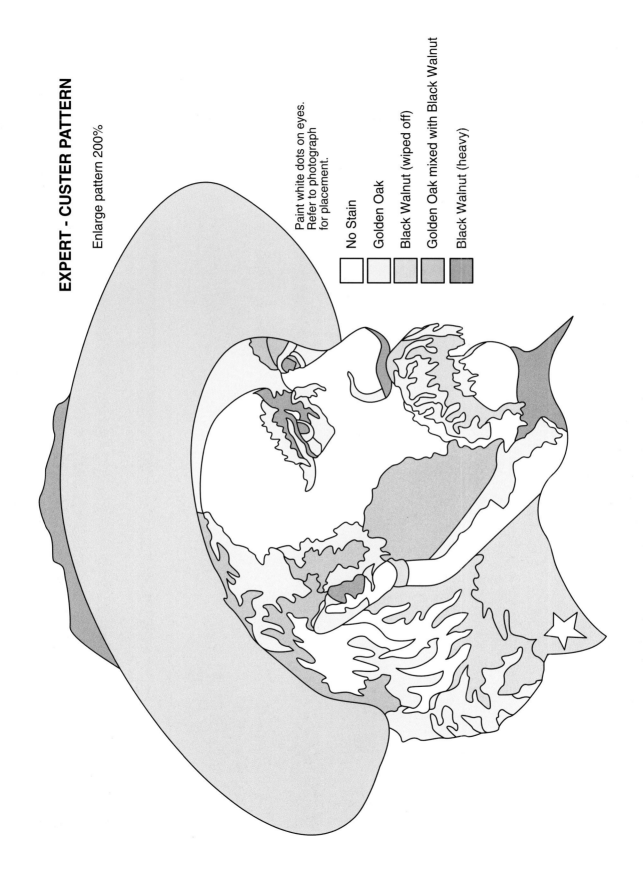

Paint white dots on eyes.
Refer to photograph
for placement.

No Stain

Golden Oak

Black Walnut (wiped off)

Golden Oak mixed with Black Walnut

Black Walnut (heavy)

Enlarge pattern 200%

No Stain

Golden Oak

Black Walnut (wiped off)

Golden Oak mixed
with Black Walnut

Black Walnut (heavy)

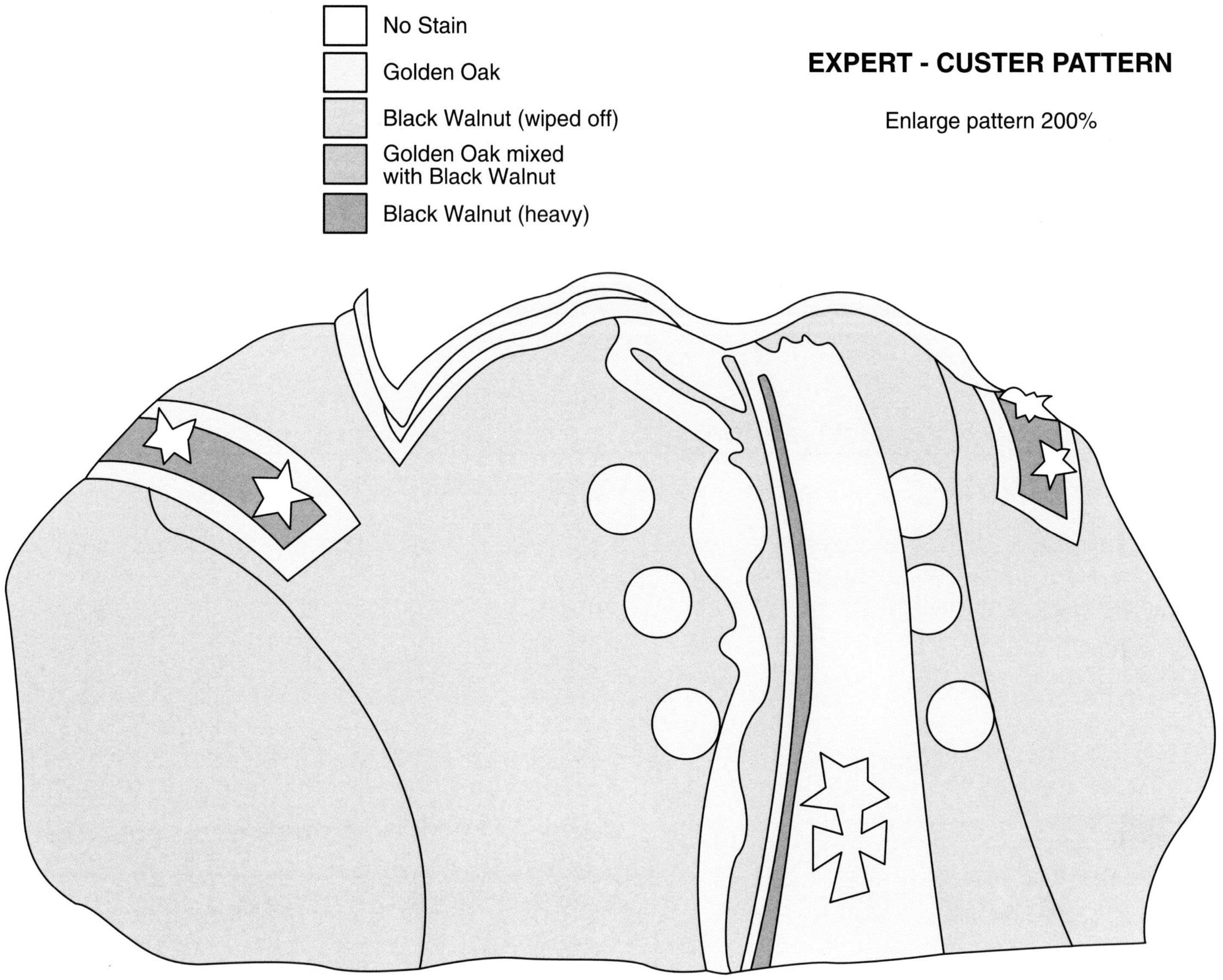

Expert - Indian Elder (Storyteller)

I call this fellow the storyteller. He knows the score, and it would be wonderful to sit with him for days just listening to him distill his wisdom. The size of the indian is 16" tall.

I try to make portraits life size, which is usually 7" from the top of the forehead to the bottom of the chin. This size allows you to cut all the unique features in the face (above), making it look like who it is supposed to look like.

The key to making this piece realistic is to give it very strong contrasts in colors and hues. The technical term for this is chiaroscuro, meaning a conjunction, a joining yet contrasting of light and dark. The effect will be electrifying and dramatic.

The terrific effect of the light shining on him is due to to how you stain the individual pieces. Blend stains while still wet to achieve the best contrast.

EXPERT - INDIAN ELDER (Storyteller) PATTERN

Enlarge pattern 153%

Paint white dots on eyes. Refer to photograph for placement.

☐ No Stain
☐ Golden Oak
☐ Golden Oak mixed with Black Walnut
☐ Red Mahogany
☐ Black Walnut (heavy)

EXPERT - INDIAN ELDER (Storyteller) PATTERN

Enlarge pattern 153%

- ☐ No Stain
- ☐ Golden Oak
- ☐ Golden Oak mixed with Black Walnut
- ☐ Red Mahogany
- ☐ Black Walnut (heavy)

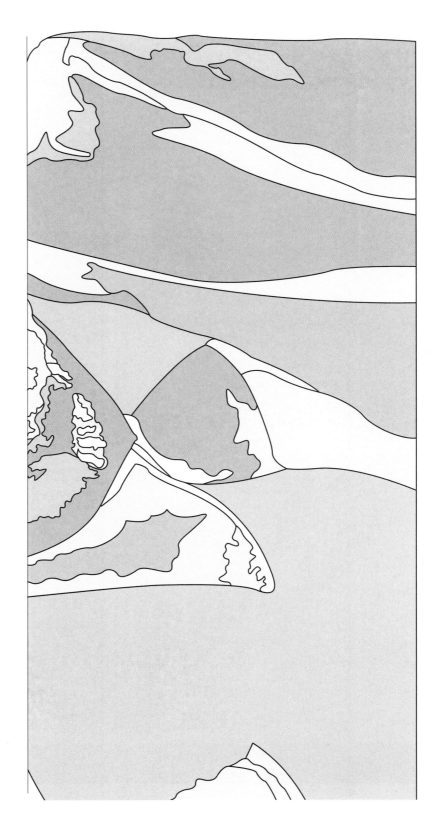

You don't have to cut each and every spot to have them appear dramatic. I combined spots frequently and they still look like individual spots.

Predrill a blade hole for each separate spot on the left side of his face. The nice thing about this is that after you stain them heavily with dark walnut, the drill holes will not show. Stain the pieces as you cut them, so that the stain can dry as you continue cutting. Keep them all together in a group so that you don't mix up spots from other areas of his body. This will make assembly infinitely easier. I also predrill the spots in his forehead as well as his eyebrows.

When I cut his chin, I cut out the spots first, stain them according to the pattern, and then cut the whiskers and the rest of the chin. Leave the whiskers unstained or stain them golden oak and wipe them off to keep them a lighter color.

The body is cut and stained a very dark golden oak. I stain it three times to deepen the golden color of his coat. The spots are stained golden oak with a mix of black walnut so that they are not as light as regular golden oak, yet not as dark as regular black walnut.

After the piece is assembled and glued, I go back and drop golden oak stain on the already stained body. This stain on stain looks like additional spots on his golden coat, and adds even more dimension.

African cats are my favorite animal to cut. This leopard will stare at you forever and never blink or flinch. This portrait technique makes the eyes look like glass. I cut this cat quite large so that details can be cut into his eyes (above). His finished size is 16" by 22". The eyes require a ³⁄₆₄" blade entry hole and all fine details are cut with a No. 2 blade. The white part of the eye is intricate and I cut it on a rather slow speed so that it can be cut in one piece.

EXPERT - LEOPARD PATTERN

Enlarge pattern 285%

Paint white dots on eyes.
Refer to photograph
for placement.

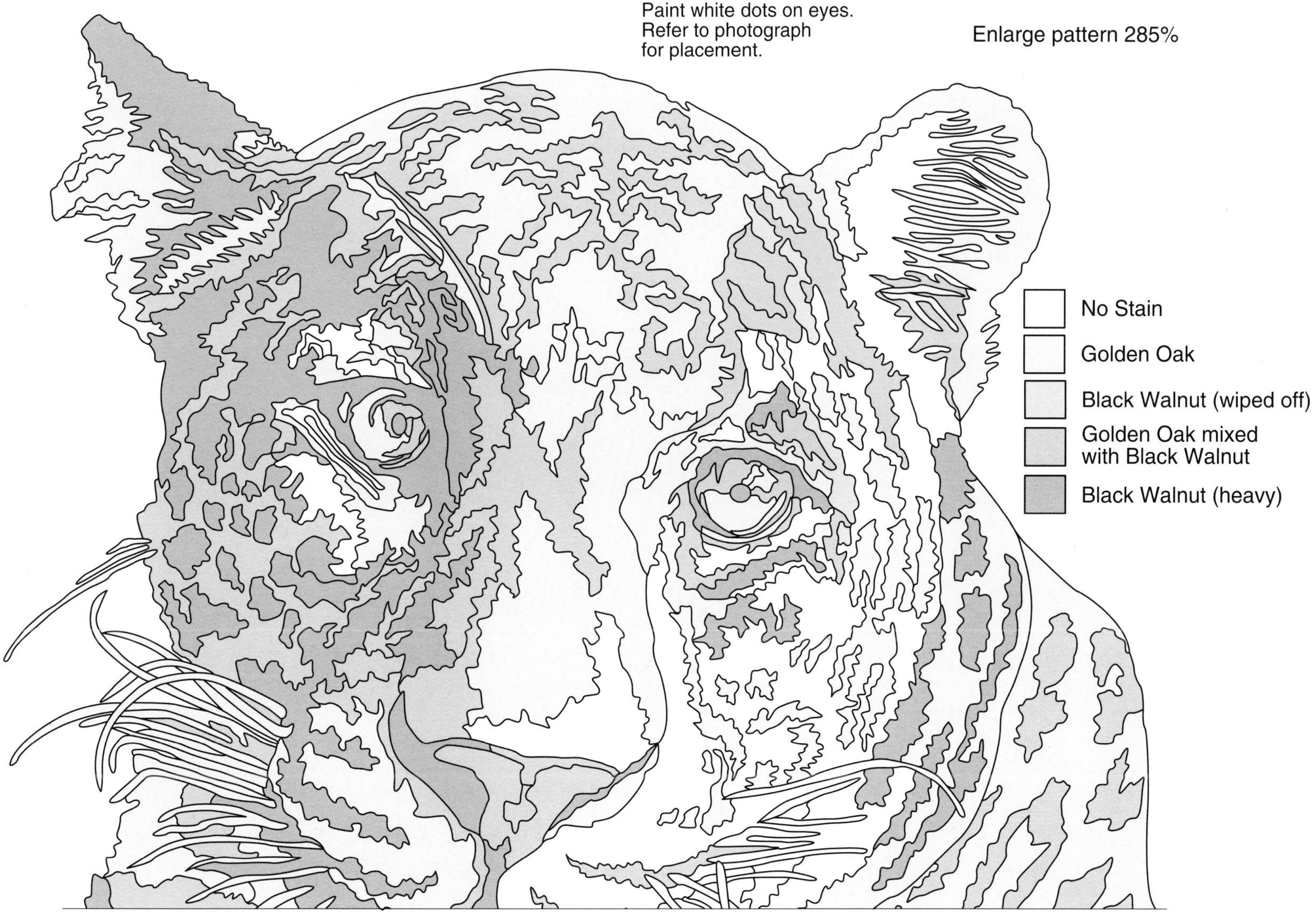

No Stain

Golden Oak

Black Walnut (wiped off)

Golden Oak mixed
with Black Walnut

Black Walnut (heavy)

EXPERT - LEOPARD PATTERN

Enlarge pattern 285%

No Stain

Golden Oak

Black Walnut (wiped off)

Golden Oak mixed with Black Walnut

Black Walnut (heavy)

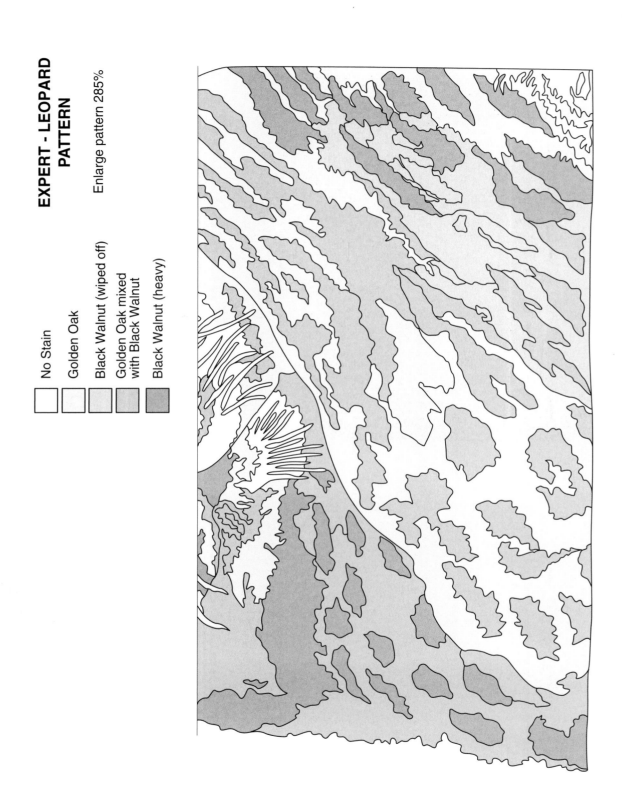

Lane

Suzie

Freedom Arms 1

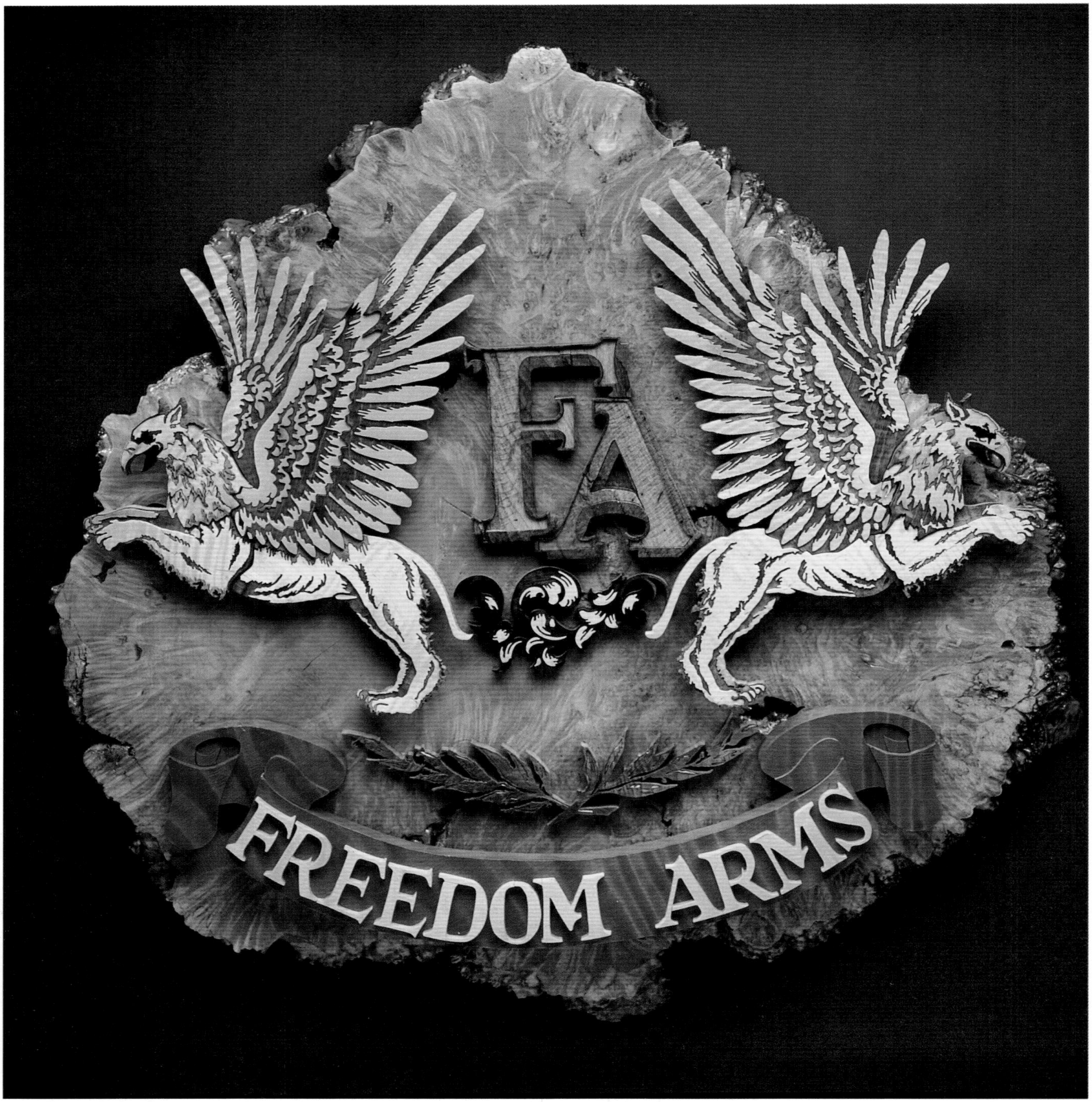

*Freedom
Arms 2*

*Freedom
Arms 3*

Colored Duck

Vertical Flying Eagle II

Sailing Ship

Standing
Ram

Indian Warrior

Cougar

Indian Princess I

Indian Princess II

Indian Elder
(Storyteller)

Answered Prayer

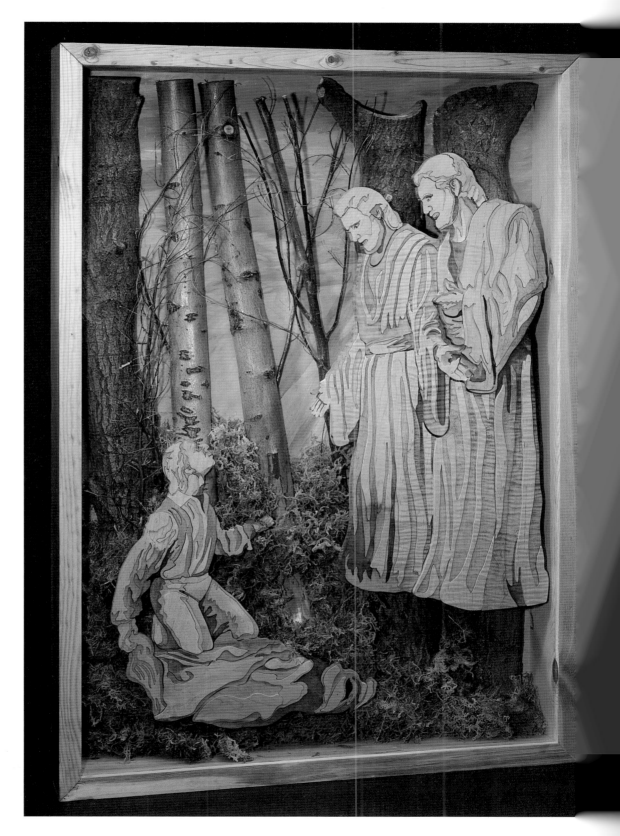

Brigham Young

John
Wayne

Bird of Prey

Thirtieth Anniversary

Mounted Wolf

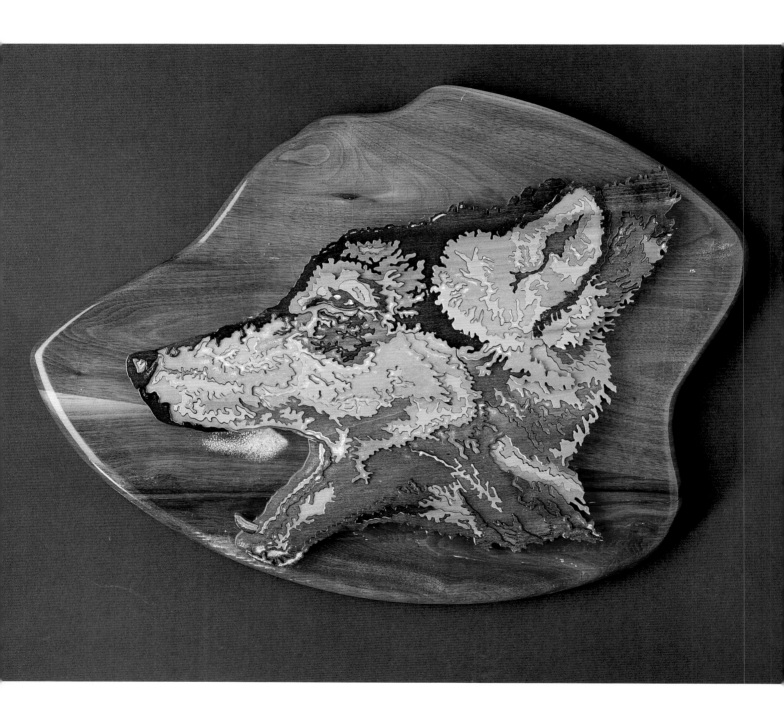

Mayan Table

Mayan
Table –
Top View

Mayan Table – Detail

Metric Equivalency Chart

inches to millimetres and centimetres
mm–millimetres   cm–centimetres

inches	mm	cm	inches	cm	inches	cm
1/8	3	0.3	9	22.9	30	76.2
1/4	6	0.6	10	25.4	31	78.7
3/8	10	1.0	11	27.9	32	81.3
1/2	13	1.3	12	30.5	33	83.8
5/8	16	1.6	13	33.0	34	86.4
3/4	19	1.9	14	35.6	35	88.9
7/8	22	2.2	15	38.1	36	91.4
1	25	2.5	16	40.6	37	94.0
1 1/4	32	3.2	17	43.2	38	96.5
1 1/2	38	3.8	18	45.7	39	99.1
1 3/4	44	4.4	19	48.3	40	101.6
2	51	5.1	20	50.8	41	104.1
2 1/2	64	6.4	21	53.3	42	106.7
3	76	7.6	22	55.9	43	109.2
3 1/2	89	8.9	23	58.4	44	111.8
4	102	10.2	24	61.0	45	114.3
4 1/2	114	11.4	25	63.5	46	116.8
5	127	12.7	26	66.0	47	119.4
6	152	15.2	27	68.6	48	121.9
7	178	17.8	28	71.1	49	124.5
8	203	20.3	29	73.7	50	127.0

yards to metres

yards	metres	yards	metres	yards	metres	yards	metres	yards	metres
1/8	0.11	2 1/8	1.94	4 1/8	3.77	6 1/8	5.60	8 1/8	7.43
1/4	0.23	2 1/4	2.06	4 1/4	3.89	6 1/4	5.72	8 1/4	7.54
3/8	0.34	2 3/8	2.17	4 3/8	4.00	6 3/8	5.83	8 3/8	7.66
1/2	0.46	2 1/2	2.29	4 1/2	4.11	6 1/2	5.94	8 1/2	7.77
5/8	0.57	2 5/8	2.40	4 5/8	4.23	6 5/8	6.06	8 5/8	7.89
3/4	0.69	2 3/4	2.51	4 3/4	4.34	6 3/4	6.17	8 3/4	8.00
7/8	0.80	2 7/8	2.63	4 7/8	4.46	6 7/8	6.29	8 7/8	8.12
1	0.91	3	2.74	5	4.57	7	6.40	9	8.23
1 1/8	1.03	3 1/8	2.86	5 1/8	4.69	7 1/8	6.52	9 1/8	8.34
1 1/4	1.14	3 1/4	2.97	5 1/4	4.80	7 1/4	6.63	9 1/4	8.46
1 3/8	1.26	3 3/8	3.09	5 3/8	4.91	7 3/8	6.74	9 3/8	8.57
1 1/2	1.37	3 1/2	3.20	5 1/2	5.03	7 1/2	6.86	9 1/2	8.69
1 5/8	1.49	3 5/8	3.31	5 5/8	5.14	7 5/8	6.97	9 5/8	8.80
1 3/4	1.60	3 3/4	3.43	5 3/4	5.26	7 3/4	7.09	9 3/4	8.92
1 7/8	1.71	3 7/8	3.54	5 7/8	5.37	7 7/8	7.20	9 7/8	9.03
2	1.83	4	3.66	6	5.49	8	7.32	10	9.14

Index